BREAK FREE

Design a Life of Financial Freedom

Jocelyn Kaufman

ISBN: 9798376690741

Cover design by: Kristianto Raharja
Library of Congress Control Number: 2023900929
Printed in the United States of America

THIS BOOK IS DEDICATED TO:

Thank you to everyone who has helped me on my journey to financial freedom.

Brady: Thank you for always pushing me to work hard and advance my position in life. You always motivate me to work harder and be a better person. I am so grateful to have you by my side.

Mom: Thank you for raising me to be independent from a young age. You have taught me so many valuable lessons that I cherish. You are a massive reason I became the person I am today.

DOWNLOAD THE FREE ONLINE WORKBOOK

To go along with this book, you can download a free fillable PDF on my website. The PDF will allow you to keep track of your notes and goals all in one place.

◆ ◆ ◆

YOU CAN ACCESS THE PDF HERE:
www.joceyj.com/breakfreereader

◆ ◆ ◆

I hope you enjoy!

- Jocelyn

CONTENTS

INTRODUCTION: SOMEDAY IS NOW

The stars will never align, and the traffic lights of life will never all be green at the same time. The universe doesn't conspire against you, but it doesn't go out of its way to line up the pins either. Conditions are never perfect. "Someday" is a disease that will take your dreams to the grave with you. Pro and con lists are just as bad. If it's important to you and you want to do it eventually, just do it and correct course along the way.

—Timothy Ferriss (author of The 4-Hour Work Week)

I had a somewhat average childhood. My family life taught me the important traits of having both unconditional love and independence. In a large and somewhat unorthodox family of nine siblings, I grew up understanding that family is not always who you share genetics with; family is unconditional love for those who are there for you through all of your ups and downs.

My mom was and still is an amazing woman. She was always a hard worker and raised me to be independent. She worked two jobs most of my childhood and on the weekdays I did not get to see her often, so my sisters and I learned to take care of our daily needs on our own.

Although I understood the meaning of unconditional love, I also understood that sometimes it came with a measure of heartbreak, and this lesson ultimately empowered me to become the strong, confident person I am today. My biological dad had passed away when I was seven years old, so my stepdad helped my mom to raise me. As I was growing up, while my mom was at work, my stepdad was always at home. He struggled with alcohol abuse and although I have amazing memories with him, they are sometimes tainted by the bad memories of when he was drunk.

Often as a child I would get overwhelmed with emotions of sadness and wish that I was living a different life. From a young age, I had to learn hard lessons and really think about what I wanted for myself. I believe that the challenges I faced as a child gave me the drive and work ethic to accomplish great things in life. I also was very lucky to have people around me that supported me and helped me along the way: My mom, grandparents, and softball coaches all played a crucial role in my childhood.

My whole life, all I wanted was to grow up, have a job, and a "normal" family. Everything I did as a child was to set myself up for the life I wanted. I started playing softball when I was five years old, and like many young athletes, my childhood quickly became consumed by the sport. As I strove to make the most of my softball career, I learned the value of hard work from an early age. I always made sure to get good grades and I worked my butt off in softball because I knew softball would one day pay for my college.

Finally, just as I had planned, I became a young adult and went to college on a softball scholarship. I did everything I could to be great in college; I double majored, I was a tutor, and I even received the most outstanding student award for my department in my senior year. After getting my bachelor's degree, I eventually went on to get my master's degree.

My dream was to graduate college, move back home, get a job, and work until retirement. So, I did just that. After getting my degree, I moved back home and applied for different high school teaching jobs. Then, I found the perfect job as a health teacher and a head softball coach at a local high school. I was excited and ready to start this new chapter in my life.

I was living the "American Dream." I was where most people dream to be in life. I had a great career as a teacher, health insurance, a 401k, and a pension. I had my master's diploma hanging on my wall and my teaching license hanging right beside it.

My enthusiasm began to dwindle. On the third day of teacher orientation, waking up at 6:00 am, I asked myself, "What am I doing?" It took me three days to realize I did not want to do this work for 40 years, especially not in the same job. I knew I wanted out and so I instantly started looking for my path out of the "American Dream." I started to learn everything I could to make it so that one day I could live a financially free life.

In this book, I describe the five life-changing steps to financial freedom that I studied and used as I began the journey to financial freedom. Now four years later, my real estate has snowballed into 52 units, bringing me $15,000 in passive income every month.

Looking back, I never felt as if I was living my "dream" life until I found financial freedom. I ultimately found my dream by taking the five life-changing steps to financial freedom. I am now a real estate agent and I help others find success in real estate as I have. My vision is to continue this journey, to make a much bigger impact in more lives, to help as many people as possible reach and achieve their own dreams. This book is the product of that vision.

My hope is that you learn as much from this book as I did along my journey. This book is for the people who want out of the W2 job, the people who want to travel the world, and the people who want to be their own boss.

This book is intended as a guide to help and motivate you toward finding your path to financial freedom. As you read about my experiences, failures and successes, I hope you will be inspired to begin your journey.

Be sure to download the free Online Workbook included with this book (you can download it at www.joceyj.com/breakfreereader) and try to apply each chapter to your own life as much as possible. Once you finish this book you should be on your way to creating your own financial freedom and I will be proud to be a small part of that.

Many people live their lives with a "someday" attitude. *Someday I'll start managing my money better. Someday I'll lose those extra 10 pounds. Someday, I'll be motivated to improve my life.* As we learned from Tim Ferriss, "someday" is a disease that can stifle our progress.

This someday mentality is a very common thinking pattern among us humans and we often use it as an excuse throughout life. You need to stop waiting for "someday". Don't wait until tomorrow. Instead, start right now.

I hope you learn a lot on your journey through *Break Free: Design a life of Financial Freedom.* Never be content with "someday" thinking. Remember to always dream, but take a hold of your dreams and make them happen. You can do this. And cheers to an early retirement!

This book is divided into five sections of foundational principles that can help prepare you for building a life of financial freedom.

5 Principles of Financial Freedom:

Section 1: Find Your WHY. You have to know your WHY. Otherwise, you will not have the motivation to succeed.

Section 2: Live Healthy. You must have good mental, physical, and social health on your journey to financial freedom.

Section 3: Gain Knowledge. You must have knowledge about your work, business interests, and skills to be successful. You also should always strive to learn more as you obtain new information that will help you on your journey.

Section 4: Money Management. You must be able to make money, save money, budget money, and build a good credit score to become financially free.

Section 5: Create Passive Income. You must create passive income through entrepreneurship, real estate, or investments. Then you will truly have financial freedom.

SECTION 1: FIND YOUR WHY

Principle 1: Find Your WHY. You have to know your WHY. Otherwise, you will not have the motivation to succeed.

CHAPTER 1: FIND YOUR WHY

Your work is going to fill a large part of your life, and the only way to be truly satisfied is to do what you believe is great work. And the only way to do great work is to love what you do.

-Steve Jobs, founder of Apple

In 2017, I graduated from college and started looking for my "dream" job. Ever since I was a 14-year-old kid, I wanted to grow up and become a high school health teacher and a head high school softball coach. I interviewed for a few different teaching jobs, then soon after my search started, I was offered the perfect job. The job was everything I wanted, so I accepted the position immediately and began planning for my first day on the job. My new job began with a new teacher orientation program that started two weeks prior to school.

On the third day of teacher orientation, a teacher came to present her classroom procedures to the new teachers. She seemed very passionate about teaching as she was showing us how she runs her classroom. At the end of the lesson, she mentioned that she had been teaching for 20 years and could not wait for retirement in another 20 years. Then it dawned on me. *This teacher has been teaching for 20 years and still has 20 years left...that's 40 years.* That is a long time to do one job your entire life. I asked myself: *Jocelyn, what are you doing? Do you really want to do this for the rest of your life? Do you really want to work for 40 years to make pennies on the dollar?*

Yep, you guessed it... I did not.

I decided at that moment that I was going to think of my teaching career as a temporary career. While working, I would use my job to save up as much money as possible. I figured I could grow my passive income to replace my teacher's salary in the first ten years of teaching. Then, once I replaced my teaching income, I would be able to retire. I understood that I could have a lot more freedom in my life if I could create enough passive income to leave my W2 job behind.

It was on that third day of teacher orientation, I found my WHY:

To create passive income so I could have financial freedom throughout my life.

I had no idea how I was going to create passive income or where I would even start, but I knew that it was going to happen.

At first, all I needed to know was my WHY.

To do anything great in life, you must have a purpose.

Your WHY is just that; your WHY is your purpose. Your WHY can be your motivation to get up in the morning, the reason you get things done, or on the flip side, it can be the reason you sit down on the couch all day wishing you were better. Your WHY can help or hurt you. If you have no dreams in life, quite simply, you will never accomplish anything significant. So, believe me when I say, identifying your WHY is critical.

Your WHY is an idea, and your WHY will always alter and change as you grow. Your WHY will be different at all stages of life, but it is essential to recognize what your WHY is in each stage. If you want to be successful, you MUST know WHY you are on this earth. If you have no purpose, then you need to sit down, think really hard, and find a reason, find a purpose, find your WHY.

It's important to understand that your WHY can be whatever you want it to be. Your WHY doesn't necessarily need to be about financial freedom. It can be to provide a better life for your child, to be able to spend more time with your family, or to be able to travel throughout your life.

It's also important to be aware that you are able to change your WHY throughout your journey. Maybe something significant will happen in your life like having a child that changes your WHY. If you have a child, you are no longer creating financial freedom strictly for yourself but for your child as well. It is inevitable that your WHY will change as your circumstances change.

Now you are going to find your WHY. I will help guide you to identify things that are important to you and help you to find what you want out of life. Then you will use that information to come up with your WHY. Make sure you take a moment to really sit down and think about your purpose and find your WHY.

Find Your Why

Find what is important to you:

1. What brings you joy?

2. If you had all the money in the world, what would you spend your time doing?

3. What activities do you love doing?

List the five most important things to you:

(Ex. Family, love, trust, sports, work, writing, reading, pets, people, etc.)

1.

2.

3.

4.

5.

3. Write a few sentences on what you want out of life:

What do you want out of life? Do you want a family? A job you love? Do you want to travel the world? Do you want financial freedom?

4. Define your WHY:

Look at all of your answers and find common ground. What is your purpose in life? What would make you happy and get you up in the morning? Then write your WHY below.

CHAPTER 2: GETTING STARTED

All who have accomplished great things have had a great aim, have fixed their gaze on a goal which was high, one which sometimes seemed impossible.

—Orison Swett Marden

On that third day of teacher orientation, I saw through the BS. I saw through the idea that everyone has to work until they are 60—ultimately for someone else's benefit. While I understood that our economy needs people to work in order to run properly, I did not want to be one of those people. I couldn't stop thinking about it. I knew I wanted more out of life.

My heart goes out to those who work manual labor their whole lives and I am very grateful that they exist, but I wanted to take a different route for myself. I had grown up watching my mom work two jobs 7 AM-10 PM every day of her life, and I saw my uncle working construction day in and day out for a company—both making almost nothing for their hard work. I noticed that the people who were making most of the money were not the ones doing the work, they were the owners, telling those people to do the work.

I knew this was not the life I wanted to live. After the third day of teacher orientation was over, I went home and came up with a plan, determined that I would create a career path that would, in the end, serve me—and serve my WHY.

First, I wrote down the amount $3,000. This was my monthly net earnings as a teacher, and that's where it all started. I looked at that number for a while, thinking to myself, "That is a lot of money." At that time in my life this was my first real job and for sure the biggest paycheck I have ever received.

Next, I wrote down all my expenses and created a budget for each category. I decided that I was going to save $2,000 each month, no excuses, and I did just that.

My Monthly Budget:

Income: $3,000
Teacher Income: $3,000

Expenses: $1000
Rent: $300

Food: $200

Gas: $200

Gym: $100

Other: $200

Total Monthly Savings: $2,000

To ensure that I could tuck these savings away and eliminate the temptation to dip into them, I opened a savings account at a new bank so that I had no checking or credit account attached to it. I figured if I did this, I could put money in but it would be more inconvenient to withdraw from my new savings. Each time I received my paycheck I immediately transferred $2,000 into my new off-limits savings account.

I am not going to lie: It was not easy to save the majority of my paycheck each month. Some months it was super easy, but other months I had to miss out on some activities I wanted to do because it was just not in my budget. I used my WHY as motivation in these moments, to save money even when I felt I was missing out on something I really wanted to do. Each time I was tempted to go on a vacation or go out to eat with friends, I reminded myself of my end goal and the temptation slowly dwindled.

Finding Motivation

Your Why- As you can tell it quickly became a nightmare of mine to have to work for corporate America my whole life. I see people every Monday say, "I cannot wait until the weekend!" It seems to me that most people just live for the weekends and therefore are missing out, essentially wasting, the other five days of the week. Don't they realize they can be free? My WHY was to create passive income so I could retire early and have financial freedom throughout my life—freedom from a job and freedom from a boss telling me what to do all the time. I made my WHY the motivation to work hard for a few years, and now I see a future I never thought was possible.

I am happy that I am not confined to working Monday through Friday 9-5 year after year, until I can finally retire at 60. I get to decide if I work and I get to choose what I do with my time.

To get anywhere in life, you have to be willing to make some sacrifices. This is not going to be easy, and sometimes you will want to quit and work the traditional 9-5 job for the rest of your life, but you have to push through those negative thoughts. Use your WHY as motivation to help you succeed. When you want to quit, think of your WHY and find a way to push through the adversity.

There are so many ways you can find motivation. You just have to find what is going to motivate you the most. You can gain inspiration from many different things or you just use your WHY as inspiration. It all depends on you and what is going to give you the most motivation.

Checklists – I love checklists and I use them in just about every facet of my life. Each time you get to check a task you completed it motivates you to get another task completed. Checklists also are a great way to stay on task and make sure you finish everything that needs to be completed.

I use checklists to keep track of my tasks but also as motivation. With any job or goal, when you just look at the big picture it can be overwhelming, but as soon as you break it down into a checklist, it becomes more attainable. Now you can complete that goal one small task at a time.

Visual Cues – Do you have a picture, favorite quote, or article that inspires you? Any of these items can be used as motivation and help you through hard times when you want to quit. You can hang your visual que on the wall or just have it in a drawer or in a book you can open when needed.

I use visual ques all the time; in fact, my background image on my phone is a motivational quote "It's hard to beat a person who never gives up." I also have a note on my phone with different quotes and goals that I reference occasionally. Once you have a visual cue that gives you motivation, you can always look at it when you feel like giving up.

Motivational Buddy – Having someone who is holding you accountable will increase the likelihood that you'll complete the task at hand. Your motivational buddy can be a friend, family member, or significant other. Tell them your goals and keep them posted on how you are doing. Now that someone other than you knows about your goal, you will be more likely to complete it.

Goal Setting

If you never have goals or any dreams, you will never accomplish anything in life. If you do not dream, you will never be anything more than you are now and you will never reach your full potential in life. We all have goals and dreams, but most people do not recognize their goals or even strive to fulfill their goals.

I use goals throughout my life to keep me on track. Each year, I make a few different goals at the beginning of the year. I make goals I can stick to and I make sure my goals are something I need to achieve. Your goals don't all need to be about financial freedom. With my yearly goals, I try to make a goal for health, finance, and giving.

I also have monthly goals I create and try to accomplish each month. Also, any time I come across a challenge in life I typically start with a goal. You do not always need to write your goals down, but you should always recognize them and come up with a plan to accomplish them.

Your goals can also be used as motivation. Anytime you create a goal, try your hardest to achieve that goal, and when you feel like giving up, push yourself to keep going. There will be goals in life that you do not reach but as long as you gave your best effort, I guarantee there will be positive effects as a result of trying.

There are two types of goals: short-term and long-term. Short-term goals are those that you can achieve within a year; long-term goals are those that take more than a year to achieve. Make sure you have both short-term and long-term goals. Also, your long-term goals should have short-term goals within them.

For example, someone striving for financial freedom may have a long-term goal of Creating $10,000 monthly passive income in five years and a short-term goal for that would be to buy an investment property by the end of the year that makes $500 a month.

It is important to set goals that matter to us, but they also need to be structured. In other words, they need to be SMART. SMART goals encompass everything that a goal should include. If you are not able to define all these categories within your goal, then your goal will become vague and ineffective.

Smart Goals:

S - Specific (What exactly do you want to accomplish?)

M - Measurable (How are you going to measure it?)

A - Achievable (How will you achieve your goal?)

R -Realistic (Is your goal realistic? However, do not be afraid to create a goal a little bit out of reach.)

T - Time (When will you complete this goal? What is the time frame?)

Now you will practice setting two SMART goals. I want you to create a short-term goal for something you want to accomplish this month, and then you will create a long-term goal for something you want to accomplish in five years. You get pretend bonus points if your goal has to do with passive income and early retirement!

Create two goals on the next two pages!

Create a SMART goal for something you want to accomplish this month (short-term goal):

Write the goal in one sentence:

Write how your goal will meet each category:

S - Specific:

M- Measurable:

A- Achievable:

R-Realistic:

T- Time:

Next, create a SMART goal for something you want to accomplish in five years (Long-term goal):

Now, write the goal in one sentence:

Write how your goal will meet each category:

S - Specific:

M- Measurable:

A- Achievable:

R-Realistic:

T- Time:

SECTION 2: LIVE HEALTHY

Principle 2: Live Healthy. You must have good mental, physical, and social health on your journey to financial freedom.

CHAPTER 3: HEALTH MATTERS

All humans are entrepreneurs not because they should start companies but because the will to create is encoded in human DNA.

— *Reid Hoffman, co-founder of LinkedIn*

T his is a book about designing your life for financial freedom. So why is there a whole section on health, you wonder? Because health plays a crucial role in the design of your life as a whole. If you are not healthy you might, one day, find success. However, you will never truly be happy. No doubt the world is full of unhealthy scoundrels who managed to achieve success, but chances are, they were simply lucky, or they are miserable and may not even live long enough to see the fruits of their labor. Why not stack the odds in your favor from the beginning and make a commitment to good health?

Being healthy takes dedication. Health is not just how you look or if you have to go to the doctor for an illness.

Health can be anything mental, social, or physical. Health is a lifelong practice. It's okay to slip up occasionally, but your overall goal should be living a healthy life. Just like we dedicate ourselves to work, we need to dedicate ourselves to being healthy. The truth is, being healthy is one of the most important things in life, so you should take your health seriously. You only get one body, and once that body is all used up, you will not exist on this earth anymore.

Before you go on this journey to financial freedom you must get your health in check. This journey is not going to be easy, and you will have a lot of obstacles that you will face. If you are not healthy, then your chances of financial success will be limited.

Here is an example of why each pillar of health is important for your journey to financial freedom:

Mental Health: You need your mind to make business deals and analyze numbers. Also, you have to be mentally tough, understand how to relieve stress, and have confidence.

Physical Health: You need your body for physical labor. If you are not eating well and exercising, you will not be able to keep up with the demands of the challenges you will face on your journey.

Social Health: You must know how to connect with people and how to properly communicate. Building strong relationships is one of the most important tools you can have on this journey to financial freedom.

CHAPTER 4: SOCIAL HEALTH

No matter how brilliant your mind or strategy, if you're playing a solo game, you'll always lose out to a team.

— *Reid Hoffman, LinkedIn co-founder*

Nobody becomes successful on their own; they are consistently moving forward, making meaningful connections with people in their industry or business. While the initial inspiration may belong to the individual, most people get where why are because they were helped, encouraged, and promoted by others. In other words, YOU will inevitably be the product of your tribe—or your team.

I use the term "team" loosely here. Your team can be anyone—it can be your mom, your high school chemistry teacher, or even your dog. It can even be a significant resource that informs your journey.

Along my journey, I realized fairly quickly that I was not

going to find success in a bubble, even if I wanted to pat myself on the back and take a well-deserved break. There's always more to do, more to learn, and more networking that needs to happen to push a plan into effective motion.

When I started out, I had saved $2,000 a month for six months and had amassed $12,000 in my bank account —an amount that seemed like a fortune at the time. I seriously thought I was rich. I could not believe it: I, Jocelyn Kaufman had $12,000 in my bank account! I was proud of myself. I did it—all on my own.

"Well, that's it," I thought to myself. "I am rich." Looking back now, I realize my reaction was both naïve and brilliant at the same time. While I was far from rich, I was quite simply *on to something,* and that something was going to certainly point me in the right direction and lay the groundwork for acquiring and maintaining wealth— but I needed to keep the momentum.

I needed a solid plan, and I needed help.

I knew I wanted to start with real estate because I had heard good things about it as a long-term investment, and it also happened that I needed a place to live. Necessity is a great motivator. Also, I had seen other people create financial freedom through real estate so it seemed like a realistic and plausible place to start.

I got on a forum called BiggerPockets (A real estate group filled with beginners and experts in real estate) and started asking questions and building connections with people. I found out that there were three things I needed to do before I could pursue a real estate purchase:

1. Find a realtor

2. Find a lender

3. Find a title company

When looking for a realtor, I knew it was important to not only find someone who had experience investing in real estate, but also someone I could connect with. I felt that it was important to trust my realtor and know that they wanted what was best for me.

I reached out to a few different realtors and had conversations with them about what I was looking for. When talking to the realtors I asked them the following questions:

1. What is your experience in real estate investing?

2. What tools and resources do you provide as a real estate agent?

3. Do you have any reviews from past clients?

After interviewing the realtors, I picked the realtor who fit my needs the best. The realtor I worked with had a fourplex and was conversational and easy to like. I built a great connection with him right from the start.

The realtor and I sat down and discussed what I was looking for and at this time I had no idea, but my realtor walked me through it. I instantly felt that my realtor would make sure I was going to get into a good deal. The connection this realtor and I made on this first deal has been the foundation of a very strong business relationship.

We looked at probably 30 duplexes and they were all way out of my price range, and I only had $12,000 to spend. I had to get creative, so I started looking for single-family homes with a separate entrance to the basement so I could possibly turn it into a mother-in-law apartment.

I opened my search engine one day and there it was. I clicked on the listing and instantly I knew this was going to be my first investment. My realtor and I went and looked at the property and my realtor reminded me that it was going to be a lot of work and I needed to make sure I was up for the task. I enthusiastically assured him that I was. I was thinking, "How hard can it be? I've watched hundreds of hours of HGTV. I got this."

I sat down and talked with my realtor about what I should offer, then we sent the offer to the sellers. After a few days, my realtor contacted me to tell me that my offer was accepted! My journey into real estate had officially begun.

Every day it seemed like I was dealing with someone else. I was either reviewing and signing docs for the real estate deal, talking with the title company, or dealing with my lender. I knew it was important to stay on top of everything because connections are everything in real estate, and I wanted everyone to jump at an opportunity to work with me again.

Finally, closing had come and I had built strong relationships with everyone involved and they were all eager to work with me again on my future deals. My hard work had paid off: It wouldn't be long before those future deals came along, and I had a head start because of connections I had made on my very first deal.

Social health is so important in finding financial freedom because you need relationships and connections to be successful. In this deal, I had to have many conversations, work with a lot of different people, and trust that they all had my best interest at heart. Being able to make good connections along the way is a huge reason why I have found so much success.

Social Health

Social health is often forgotten when someone is striving for financial freedom. Social health is being able to form strong relationships with others and to be able to have positive social interactions. I had to create strong relationships in that first real estate deal to make it a smooth process. People often view social health, especially personal social health, as a deterrent to success, but it is the opposite. Having good social health positively affects your ability to be successful.

Not only that, but social health can have a tremendous impact on your personal life as well. Poor social health has been linked to health problems such as heart disease, high blood pressure, and other chronic health conditions. Research has shown that poor social health leading to loneliness can be worse for your health than a lifetime of smoking (Tiwari 2013). While hard work is a key ingredient to success, it's not healthy to overwork yourself. You still need to take some time with your family and friends. Throughout my journey to financial freedom, I have always made sure to make time for my family and friends no matter how busy I have gotten.

In order to find financial freedom, you must have good social health. Social health will make you more confident, give you higher self-esteem, and you will be able to form and build relationships—all of which are important in your journey to financial freedom.

Social Interactions

If you feel stressed, overworked, or just need to have some fun, social interactions with others will make you feel a lot better and increase your overall social health. There are so many different opportunities to have social interactions and it is important to find a few you enjoy.

Within your work - The reality is, a majority of people spend most of their time with people they work with. Your coworkers can become your closest friends. It is easy to look at your coworkers as just coworkers, but if you become friends with your coworkers you are more likely to enjoy your work. A lot of workplaces will have activities and different company events. You can use these as an opportunity to create some friendships with your coworkers.

Examples of work social interactions:
- Each lunch with a coworker.
- Attend work parties and events.
- Chat with your coworkers on breaks.
- Go to dinner with your coworkers after work.

Join a club – There is a club for just about anything. If you are interested in something why not surround yourself with others who are interested in the same thing? The reason alcoholics go to AA is so they have a support system, and they are around people that are going through the same thing. Whether it's hobbies, sports, or support groups, it is essential to be surrounded by people who share your interests.

Examples of club social interactions:
- Sewing club
- Group fitness club
- Adult softball team
- Cooking club
- Book club
- Bunco club

Spend time with your family and friends – When striving for success, many people view spending time with family and friends as a deterrent to success. The perception is that when you are spending time with these people and not at work, you are not advancing. No matter how successful and busy you get, always make time for your family and friends because these people will always be there for you.

Examples of family and friends social interactions:
- Meet them for dinner or lunch.
- Have them over for a game night.
- Go do something fun together as a group.
- Attend your family and friends' events that your

invited to.

The road to finding financial freedom will be stressful at times. If you ever feel stressed or overworked, you should have at least three things you can turn to in order to relieve that stress.

Write down three social activities you can go and do for fun:

1.

2.

3.

Relationships

As you know, when I was 7, my biological dad passed away. My mom remarried and my stepfather (I called him dad) helped raise me. My dad and I had a great relationship when he was not drinking. But unfortunately, he was a struggling alcoholic and most of my memories of him are tainted. I remember nights I would stay up chatting with him all night. It would always turn into a conversation telling me that I will never accomplish anything in my life, when all I ever wanted was to make him proud of me.

While my mom was at work all day and he was watching

my sisters and I, he would get angry about little things every day. As a child I constantly had to deal with mental abuse and sometimes physical abuse. As I grew older, my dad and I grew apart to a point where we never spoke. Not even a happy birthday text.

A couple of years into college he reached out to me, and we started to build our relationship again. During my senior year in college, he passed away from alcoholism and I am so grateful I forgave him and tried to love him as he was. I was able to spend some amazing moments with my dad in the two years before he passed away and I will always remember the time he said "I am proud of you" because that's all I ever wanted. If I would have never worked on our relationship, I would have never heard those words and I would be holding onto a lot of regrets.

Personal and business relationships are vital to your success. To have good social health, you need to focus on improving both types of relationships. If you want to find success one day you must be able to form and keep strong relationships, because these relationships will aid you in your success. For example, in my first deal in real estate, I had to build relationships with the realtor, the lender, the title company, etc. Later in my journey, I have had to build relationships with construction workers, property managers, tenants, and now real estate clients. Being able to create and nourish strong relationships is a great tool to have on your journey to financial freedom.

Four Foundations Of A Strong Relationship

There are four foundations of a strong relationship, and all of them are needed on your journey to financial freedom. Make sure to continually try and improve in all four of these foundations:

1. Communication

Communication is needed for networking, presenting, public speaking, building relationships, and all other aspects of personal and professional development. Communicating effectively and confidently is one of the most important skills you can master.

How to be a good communicator:

Listen with an open mind: When you are listening, you should be sharing non-verbal cues like nodding your head, maintaining eye contact or smiling.

Communicate with friendliness and respect: No one wants to have a conversation with someone who seems mean or bored.

Have confidence and be clear when you speak: When you are communicating, you must be confident in yourself. When you are confident, more people will believe and trust what you are saying.

2. Trust

The next foundation of relationships is trust. Often people are guarded, and they do not trust anyone. The inability to trust is very harmful to success and your overall social health. Never go into a relationship feeling like the other person needs to earn your trust. Even if you have had bad experiences in the past, understand that everyone is different, and just because someone broke your trust in the past does not mean everyone is untrustworthy.

Trust is the glue that holds business relationships together. If you do not trust your business partner, you will spend more time worrying about protecting yourself rather than the actual business itself. You will never be successful in that business because you will spend too much time and energy wondering if your partner will stab you in the back. Distracted people often get taken advantage of.

I had a business partner once who had a bad experience in the past. In the past, he was taken advantage of financially, and it affected him tremendously. As we were working together and building the business, he was only worried about what I was doing and if I would steal from him. Instead of trusting me to do my job, he would constantly start conversations, essentially micromanaging everything I did.

This distrust made me feel very stressed because I knew my partner did not trust me. The business relationship was very rocky, and the business failed because of it. I have yet to enter into another business endeavor with this individual because I know that we will not be successful. What could have been a great business venture turned into a bad experience for everyone, all because he was unable to trust.

Tips to build trust:
- Honor your commitments
- Be vulnerable
- Be honest
- Communicate well
- Admit when you are wrong

3. Appreciation

Appreciation is essential in relationships. Each party must appreciate the other. It is easy to have high expectations in a relationship and forget to appreciate the other person for what they do and who they are. However, you must appreciate your partner to build a strong relationship. On your journey to financial freedom, you will always be dealing with others, and it is essential to know how to appreciate them.

Three ways to tell/show someone you appreciate them:
- Tell them why you appreciate them and be specific.
- Surprise your partner with something small like coffee or flowers. Actions speak louder than words.
- Write them a letter telling them why and how you appreciate them.

4. Forgiveness

Forgiveness is essential for both your social health and your ability to be successful. Plus, the act of forgiving has strong health benefits. A study at the University of Tennessee found that people who could forgive had lower blood pressure and a lower resting heart rate, versus those who have a hard time forgiving. The study also found that people who forgave easier were able to work harder to resolve conflict and had stronger relationships (Lawler et al. 2003).

Throughout your life, you will come across many circumstances where you have to practice forgiveness. These circumstances may be in personal or business relationships; sometimes you may even have to forgive yourself.

If you do not forgive, you will carry that hate and fear into other relationships. A perfect example is my business partner not trusting me due to a previous relationship that went south.

Forgiveness is essential to your own mental health; it is an act of self-care, and it's not for their benefit, but for yours. Forgiving someone does not mean you have to re-enter into that relationship. You can forgive and move on or forgive and repair the relationship. Either way, you must forgive. Your social health depends on your ability to forgive as life throws you challenges.

About a year into my journey, I found a contractor that was amazing. I had him do a few big jobs for me and he did a great job. We had built a good business relationship and I felt like I could count on him. It was very nice to have someone I could rely on when it came to my properties.

I had some big repairs coming up and he had to buy the materials so he needed half up front. He was going to repair the rain gutters on two houses, a roof, and a unit. I paid him half up front which was $14,000. Fast forward three months...I started to get after him because I needed him to get the work done, but he kept putting it off.

Suddenly, he was renting a nice house and driving a new motorcycle. At this point, I still did not think anything fishy was going on because I trusted he would do the work. One month later, I was notified that he was in jail and had stolen a total of $50,000 from his clients.

At this point in my career, $14,000 was a detrimental amount of money and I had no idea how I was going to bounce back from that. I felt so violated and hurt that someone I trusted would do that to me, but I had to move on and learn from it. I learned and responded by adopting a policy to never pay half upfront again. Although I will never work with that contractor again, I forgave the situation and found another contractor who has done great work for three years now.

Relationship Exercise

After learning about the foundations of relationships and their importance to success. I want you to list three things you can do to improve your relationships. You will do this exercise for both personal and professional relationships.

Personal Relationship:

1.

2.

3.

Professional Relationship:

1.

2.

3.

CHAPTER 5: FRAME YOUR MIND

Do not let the memories of your past limit the potential of your future. There are no limits to what you can achieve on your journey through life, except in your mind.

— *Roy T. Bennett, author*

I finally had my first property. I also only had $750 in the bank. The property needed a complete remodel and I obviously did not have money to pay for someone else to do it, so I decided to remodel the property myself. I never had done any work in construction before but it was about time I learned. Crazy? Yes. Doable? Also yes.

To learn how to do the construction I watched a lot of YouTube videos and I had some help from family members and friends. At the time, I was working a full-time teaching job, coaching softball, getting my master's degree online, remodeling this house, training for an MMA fight, and I still made time for family and friends.

I had a lot on my plate and there were a lot of different stressors I was facing. It seemed my mind was constantly assessing my situation. *Will I have enough money to pay my bills? Will I win my MMA fight? What should we do at softball practice today? I have a big test coming up, where do I find time to study?*

I had to put my head down and work hard through this time in my life. However, I also needed to take care of my mental health, so I made sure I got good night's sleep every night, practiced a ten-minute meditation each morning when I woke up, and I tried not to stress about things that I could not control.

Here was my daily schedule:
6:00 AM – Wake up and get a short 30-minute workout at home
6:30 AM – Drive to work
6:45 AM – Take a shower at work
7:00 AM – School starts
12:00 PM – Workout on my lunch break
12:30 PM – Hurry and eat lunch
12:45 PM – School resumes
3:00 PM – School ends and work on my master's degree
5:00 PM – Go to the gym and work out
6:00 PM – Go to MMA practice
8:00 PM – Go home and work on my house
10:00 PM – Go to bed

My schedule was not easy and Monday through Friday was often very rough. Even Saturdays and Sundays were devoted mostly to fixing up my house. There were days I wanted to skip MMA practice or skip the two-hour window I had to work on my house, but most days I pushed through it. There were only a few times I gave myself a break and it was because I knew I needed it. In those breaks, I focused on my social or mental health and those breaks gave me the energy to start back up the next day.

When remodeling the house, I first fixed up the upstairs unit because I knew it needed the least amount of work, and so I lived in the downstairs unit on a cement floor. All I had was a couch that had a pull-out bed, a fridge, and a microwave. There was no sheetrock or insulation and I went without a toilet for one month and a shower for two months. My routine was to shower at work or at the gym.

Finally, after a month of hard work, I finished the upstairs unit and I rented it for $1,800, including utilities. My mortgage payment was $1,200, and utilities typically stayed under $400, so I was now living for free and making $200 a month off the upstairs unit being rented. This moment in my journey was so relieving and when I realized I was going to make money off of that house it gave me a lot of motivation to keep pushing forward. Because I was making money off of the house, most of my W2 paycheck could go to repairs on the basement and I no longer had to worry about a monthly mortgage payment. Phew!

My Monthly Budget:

Income: $3,200
Teacher Income: $3,000
Cashflow 1st House: $200

Expenses: $700
Food: $200
Gas: $200
Gym: $100
Other: $200

Total Monthly Savings: $2,500

As you can guess this was a very mentally taxing time in my life. I had to make conscious, deliberate strides to take care of my mental health and stay positive. I could have quit or burned myself out on remodeling the upstairs unit but I didn't. I buckled down and got through it.

How mental health played a role in my first remodel:

1. People told me it was a lot of work and I couldn't do it.

Instead of listening to them, I put my head down and got it done. I had done enough research that I knew that I could do it.

2. Buying your first house is stressful.

Right before closing, I felt like I was going to throw up. I had to remind myself that it is going to be okay and that this was a big step to financial freedom.

3. Coming home from a long day of work to more work was mentally challenging.

I had to keep telling myself it will be worth it in the end and that once this unit is rented out, things will get easier.

Mental Health

The mind is a brilliant piece of machinery. It is capable of limitless creativity and can be one of our best allies along our road to success. Yes, indeed, your *mind* is essential to your financial freedom... and if you do not take steps to keep it healthy, this will only deter and discourage you from achieving your goals.

Unfortunately, mental health is often forgotten or not taken seriously. The mind is a very powerful tool. It can set our visions and dreams into motion, fuel our creativity, and give us unimagined success—but this power always comes with the risk of negatively impacting our mental health.

Mental health affects how we think, feel, act, and how we cope with life. You must be able to cope and deal with different stressors as they come to be mentally healthy. Had I not been mentally healthy on my first remodel, I would have failed. I would have never gotten through a challenge like that; that challenge is what started me on my journey to financial freedom.

If you decide to go on this journey, it is not easy. You will face challenges and you NEED to be mentally healthy to combat all the challenges that come your way. You can become mentally tough through self-acceptance and managing your stress.

If you are reading this book, chances are you are trying to better yourself and improve your life. Most likely, you already have the right mindset to get started. You value and understand the importance of hard work. It is especially important for you not to burn yourself out as you pursue your goals. I occasionally had to take short breaks and focus on my social or mental health and you should do the same. If you start to feel exhausted or overwhelmed, take a minute or as long as you need to get your mind right.

Self-Acceptance

Self-acceptance is loving and accepting yourself as you are. When you accept yourself, you know your worth. You value who you are and what you can do. You accept all of your personality traits, physical, and mental attributes, and you feel a sense of self self-worth.

You must love yourself—all the good parts as well as the bad. Everyone is extraordinary in their own way, and I promise you, you are remarkable. Now all you need to do is accept how great you are.

After you accept yourself as you are, you will have nothing to hide.

• You will be more confident.

• You will be less vulnerable to negative comments from others.

• You will be able to control your emotions when challenges are thrown your way.

• You will be more self-compassionate, meaning you will recognize and love yourself when you need it.

Four Steps To Self-Acceptance

1. Practice gratitude

One great way to self-acceptance is to practice self-gratitude. You should ALWAYS be kind to yourself. Love yourself for who you are, appreciate what you have and what you accomplish, and most importantly, stay true to yourself.

When you are working on a project or when you accomplish something, be proud of yourself. Make sure to celebrate all the little things because that will help get you through the tough times you will face on your journey to financial freedom.

Remember, you are the only person who can control how you think. Never self-criticize. If you mess up, learn from it and move on. If you sit there and dwell on your downfalls, you will most likely fail on your journey to financial freedom.

2. Reframe your negative thoughts

This world is filled with challenges and uncertainties that can lead to feelings of fear and discouragement. Throughout your journey, you must learn how to reframe negative thoughts. Learn to let go of things you have no control over. The only thing you have control over is your thoughts and your actions. You have zero control over anything anyone else does. Once you start focusing on your thoughts and actions, you will become a lot happier. If you have a negative thought, reframe it into something positive and use it as a learning experience.

On my first remodel I had to take down an entire wall. I sat there and stared at the wall for a while and thought to myself. "This is impossible, there is no way I can do this myself." Then, I reframed what I was thinking, "Well I might as well try, I have nothing to lose." I first took off the sheetrock and then felt like I was that much closer. Then I took off one 2x4 at a time and eventually the wall was down.

I just needed to believe I could do it.

3. Forgive yourself

You are a human, and you will make mistakes throughout your life. That is a fact. You MUST be able to forgive yourself. Just like we have to be able to forgive others in our lives, we have to forgive ourselves.

You will make mistakes on your journey to financial freedom and how you bounce back from those mistakes will determine how successful you are. When you make a mistake, let it go. Understand there is nothing you can do about it now, learn from it, and move forward.

4. Put yourself first

You should always put YOU first. Make sure to balance your personal and social time. Always set time aside for YOU. Do not be afraid to say no to things if you need some personal time. If you like to knit, set time aside in the day to knit. Suppose you enjoy reading, set time aside in the day to read. Find something that brings you joy and make time for yourself to do it.

Managing Your Stress

Stress is the body's natural reaction to prepare us for action. Stress is necessary to get humans to react to threats or challenges, but can be very harmful to your mental health. There are two types of stress: acute and chronic. Acute stress is what everyone experiences. You have a deadline or face a threat, and your body receives stress, so you meet the deadline or get away from the threat. Then there is chronic stress. Chronic stress is when stress lasts for an extended period of time. Chronic stress can be very harmful to your physical and mental health and must be dealt with.

During that first remodel, I faced a lot of stress. I had to get the upstairs unit finished so I did not have to pay the mortgage myself anymore. I managed the stress I faced and I was able to use the stress to my benefit to get the job done. I always put my mental health first and if I was exhausted and needed time to rest, I would give myself a day off.

Sleep And Stress

Sleep and stress are a double-edged sword. Getting a good night's sleep will help you combat stress, but stress can wreak havoc on the quality your sleep. It is an ongoing cycle, so you must deal with your stress and get some ZZZ's.

4 Tips to better your sleep:

- Get lots of sun early in the day.
- Recognize when you are stressed.
- Create a nightly routine.
- Get help if you struggle with sleep.

Sun Versus Stress

Sun exposure early in the day not only can help you sleep better at night but can also help you battle stress and be happier. Sun has a lot of health benefits, and it is essential to get sun exposure whenever possible. A study that followed 30,000 Swedish women revealed that those who spent more time in the sun lived six months to two years longer than those with less sun exposure (Lindqvist 2014). Get outside even if it's cold. Try and go on walks in the morning or during your lunch break. Sun exposure is so significant and will change your life when dealing with stress.

I always set aside time to go on a walk or run almost every day outside, even if it is only 15 minutes.

Get outside and get some sun!

Be Able To Cope

Half way through my basement remodel, my brother passed away. So I had to put everything on pause and worry about my family. I took two weeks off of work, stopped working on my house, and paused training for my MMA fight. My family comes first, and I needed to be there for them so I paused everything in my life that I had control over. I still had to work on my master's degree and create sub plans for my substitute at school, but I tried to free up as much time as possible for my family.

My brother lived in another state so my whole family flew out there. It was hard to know that he is gone but the saddest part was that he had two daughters. I felt so much for them because I personally know what it is like to lose your dad. My whole family gathered together and celebrated his life.

After a lot of my family left, I stayed another week to make sure my grandma was okay and my nieces were going to be okay. Then once my two weeks off of work were over, I went back to my normal life. This time was very hard to go through but I knew that I couldn't change what had happened to my brother. All I could do is try and make sure my family was okay and think of the good memories I shared with him.

At some point in your life, you will face something that will force you to cope; otherwise, the stress will eat you up inside. When you are faced with a problem, you must cope. Stay positive and understand what things you can control and what you cannot. If you let things out of your control affect you and make you stressed, you will always be stressed. If something is entirely out of your control, then try to move forward. Stay positive when faced with life's different challenges and cope with them.

Failures will happen often on your journey to financial freedom. You are not perfect and everything will not work out just the way you want it. So, when things don't work out, cope with it. Next time you are faced with a stressor. Ask yourself if it is in your control. If it is not, then do your best to move on. If it is, then stay positive and come up with a plan to combat it.

Be Thankful

Be thankful for the good things in your life. Each day you should have a specific time in the day dedicated to thinking about at least three things you are thankful for. I like to do this first thing in the morning to start my day off right. You can write down three things you are thankful for or just think about them in your head. By being thankful and practicing gratitude, your life will become a lot fuller and more meaningful.

Try it now!

Write down three things you are thankful for right now:

1.

2.

3.

Mental Wellness Practices

Here are some mental wellness practices you can use when you feel stressed. If none of these work for you, there are a ton of free resources online. Just look up mental wellness exercises online and use them when you feel stressed.

1. Deep breathing exercises

Look up a script online, or just take a minute to focus on your breath. Breathe in while pushing your stomach out, filling up your lungs, then breathe out nice and slow, sucking your stomach in. Do this over and over again while focusing only on your breath.

2. Meditation

YouTube is full of free meditation sessions. If you are new to meditation, I suggest starting there. Once you get the hang of it, you can begin to meditate on your own.

3. Progressive muscle relaxation

This is a form of meditation. This exercise will have you focus on different parts of your body and relaxing them one at a time. You can find different lessons online until you get the hang of it.

4. Journaling

Take some time to write in your journal. Write what is going well in life, what you can improve on, what you are looking forward to, etc. It is your journal. You can write about whatever you like. If you choose to write about something negative, then try and write down the positive side or how you can turn the negative into a positive.

5. Practice gratitude

Be thankful for what you have. Like the exercise we did earlier, it can be as simple as writing down three things you are grateful for.

6. Exercising

Go on a walk or do a quick workout. Exercise is critical to our physical and mental well-being, but exercising can also help you deal with stress.

My Three Favorite Daily Activities to combat stress:

1. Short meditation exercises – I try and do a least 10 minutes every morning or night while I am lying in bed.

2. Be thankful – Whenever I am driving place to place, I try and think of three things I am thankful for.

3. Exercise – I love the way I feel after I exercise so I try and get at least one 30-minute workout in each day.

Pick three activities you can try to help combat your stress:

1.

2.

3.

CHAPTER 6: GET PHYSICAL

Obstacles don't have to stop you. If you run into a wall, don't turn around and give up. Figure out how to climb it, go through it, or work around it.

— Michael Jordan, former professional basketball player

Meeting the challenges of life requires mental tenacity, but it also requires physical tenacity. The muscles in our body will atrophy if they are not used—this is a fact. Because we live in a world of fast food, conveniences, and distractions, modern humans almost certainly have to participate in some sort of focused exercise. Unless we work on a construction site or we are an Alaskan homesteader walking miles per day to harvest meat for the winter, our daily lives do not require much of us physically, so we have to compensate.

Physical health has always been an important part of my life, but even more so during my journey to financial freedom, so I quickly established a routine. I would wake up, get in a short 30-minute workout then go to work and teach. Right after school, I would have softball practice and then I would hustle to MMA practice. I would get home with about two hours to work on the downstairs renovations and then go to bed and start the process all over again.

After completing the upstairs unit, I started on the downstairs. It was easy to want to spend every moment I could working down there, because I really wanted to finish it. I was motivated to finish quickly so I could move on to the next step in my journey, but I also made sure I did it right. I insulated all the walls and ceiling, removed a wall, sheet rocked everything, expanded the bathroom, installed floors, painted everything, did electrical work, and had a washer and dryer added downstairs. I learned a lot as I did this project, and I received a lot of help from different family and friends. I never quit and there was no way I wasn't going to finish what I had started. After three months of hard work, I finally finished the basement apartment, and I then was able to start saving up some money for the next step in my journey.

By this time in my journey, it was clear that my physical health was being tested. I was doing a lot of different things and definitely burning a lot of calories. I had to make sure I was eating a proper diet, getting good sleep, exercising, and practicing good self-care.

Throughout this next section, we discuss the elements of physical health, including nutrition, exercise, and wellness, and how all of these elements are vital on your journey to financial freedom. Please keep in mind that I am not a doctor nor do I know anything about you. Please talk to your doctor about anything you decide to change in your health. This section is meant to give you a good source of information but everyone is different and you should consult your doctor before making any changes.

Nutrition

How I make sure I am physically healthy:

With my daily nutrition I try to make good choices. Over the years, I have tried to build up good nutritional habits I can stick with that increase my overall health. To me, eating healthy isn't necessarily to be skinny or have a perfect body but to provide my body with the proper nutrition to live a long healthy life.

Small nutritional habits I stick to:

- Drink a lot of water
- I rarely drink soda
- I rarely eat fast food

Everyone knows that eating healthy and drinking an adequate amount of water are very good for your health. Everyone knows that fast food, soda, and candy are bad for your health. However, the fast-food lines are always full, and the candy and soda in the store are constantly restocked. We know these things are bad for our health, but we eat them anyway. They are convenience foods, designed and marketed to entice busy, stressed and overwhelmed people. While striving for success, it is easy to forget about your physical health. Typically, when you are in success mode, you are extremely busy and do not have time to be picky about what you are eating.

When people think of healthy eating, they typically think of strict diets or constantly depriving themselves of food that tastes good. Instead, I will urge you to take some small steps to create healthy habits that lead to a better nutritional diet. Taking these small nutritional steps will make you feel better, you will have more energy, and your mental health will benefit from it as well.

I will give you a crash course on the main components of nutrition and some tips to clean up your diet. Take your nutrition seriously because it can hinder you on your journey to financial freedom if you don't.

Fats

There are healthy fats and unhealthy fats. The trick is to eat healthy fats and avoid unhealthy fats—imagine that! Fats are essential to our diet. Fats nourish your brain, your cells, your hair, skin, and nails. Fats also provide you with energy when doing low-intensity exercises like walking or other daily activities.

Healthy fat examples:

Peanut oil, olive oil, canola oil, avocado oil, avocados, nuts, seeds, Omega 3, Omega 6, fish, and oil supplements

Unhealthy fat examples:

Crackers, candies, shortenings, snack foods, fried foods, and processed foods made with hydrogenated vegetable oils

Protein

Protein is the basic building block of your body's tissues, and protein is vital to have in your body. Protein also allows metabolic reactions to take place in the body and coordinates bodily functions.

Complete protein examples:

Fish, poultry, eggs, beef, pork, dairy, and whole sources of soy (tofu, edamame, tempeh, miso).

Food combinations to get complete protein examples:

Rice and beans, peanut butter sandwich, noodles with peanuts, hummus and whole-grain pitas, fried rice with peas, and barley and lentil soup.

Do not be afraid to incorporate other types of protein into your diet other than meat. Variety is essential in the diet. You can incorporate items like beans, nuts, and soy to get extra protein into your diet.

Carbohydrates

Carbohydrates get a lot of hate in our culture, as evidenced by the popularity of low carb diets. Carbs may seem like the enemy, but in reality, our body NEEDS carbs. Carbohydrates are your body's primary source of energy. They help fuel your brain, kidneys, heart, muscles, and central nervous system.

The key is choosing the right carbs. Like fats, there are good (healthy) carbs and bad (unhealthy) carbs. Unhealthy carbohydrates will digest very quickly and cause a spike in blood sugar and energy. Unhealthy carbs will also cause inflammation in your body.

Sugar is the devil of carbohydrates, and most of the time, we do not even know we are eating it. Sugar is responsible for most health and weight problems, and it causes inflammation in the body and toxins in the brain. Avoid sugary foods and drinks and instead replace them with naturally sweet foods like fruit, peppers, or natural peanut butter.

Healthy carbohydrate examples:

Fruits, vegetables, whole grains, quinoa, brown rice, barley, and beans.

Unhealthy carbohydrate examples:

Sugar, white flour, white rice, white bread, and any carb that has been stripped of all bran fiber and nutrients also known as "processed foods."

Minerals And Vitamins

Minerals and vitamins are essential substances that our bodies need to develop and function normally. You should get all the vitamins and minerals you need through a well-balanced, nutrient-dense diet. You can take supplements, but they are not as beneficial as eating a nutrient-dense diet. When adding vitamin and mineral supplements into your diet, do it one at a time. See how it makes you feel and make sure it has a positive effect on your body.

Essential vitamins:

A, C, D, E, and K, and the B vitamins: thiamin (B1), riboflavin (B2), niacin (B3), pantothenic acid (B5), pyridoxal (B6), cobalamin (B12), biotin, and folate/folic acid

Essential minerals:

calcium, phosphorus, potassium, sodium, chloride, magnesium, iron, zinc, iodine, sulfur, cobalt, copper, fluoride, manganese, and selenium

Prebiotics And Probiotics

Prebiotics increase the diversity of your microbiome by populating your gut with bacteria. Foods rich in prebiotics feed probiotics and encourage the growth of healthy bacteria in the gut. Eating probiotics will help repopulate the bacteria in your gut. Both prebiotics and probiotics are essential to have in your daily diet.

Prebiotics:

pickles, kimchi, unprocessed yogurt, and kombucha

Probiotics:

cayenne pepper, coconut oil, garlic, ginger, lemons, limes, olive oil, onions, pumpkin seeds, and rutabaga

Water

Water is essential to our daily lives. When you are drinking enough water, you will feel a massive difference in your mind and body. According to the CDC, water helps your body keep an average temperature, lubricate and cushion joints, protect your spinal cord and other sensitive tissues, and get rid of wastes through urination, perspiration, and bowel movements. If you are in a hot climate where you are sweating a lot, exercising, or running a fever, it is crucial to up your water intake ("Physical Activity" 2022).

To find out how much water you should drink, take your body weight and divide it in half, and that is the amount of water you should drink in ounces.

Example:
Weight: 150
Divide by 2: 150/2 = 75
Water to drink daily: 75 oz

Small Steps

The best way to eat healthy is to start small. Create daily habits that you can follow to clean up your diet. Start small and practice moderation when it comes to the unhealthy foods. You can eat anything in moderation. If you love sugary foods, then allow yourself to have them sometimes.

How To Eat Healthy

"95% of everything you do is the result of habit. So the rule is to allow good habits to become your masters than let bad habits form."
– Aristotle.

10 tips for cleaning up your eating habits:

• Only allow yourself to have fast food once a week.

• If you have a delicious dessert, tell yourself, you must eat healthy the next day.

• Chew your food slowly and pay attention to every bite.

• Drink fermented or probiotic soda instead of sugary soda.

• Add a lot of leafy greens and vegetables to every meal to fill you up.

• Try not to eat in front of a tv or while reading because that can cause overeating.

• Listen to your body and understand if you are starving.

• Avoid eating too late in the night. Try eating an early dinner and then fasting until breakfast time.

• Fasting has been shown to have a lot of health benefits. An easy way to do this is to eat an early dinner and then fast through the night.

• Carry a water bottle with you throughout the day and opt for water when you are dining out.

Exercise

How I make sure I am physically healthy:

I love the way I feel after exercising, and I know how important exercise is for physical health. I try and get at least 30 minutes of some type of exercise in each day. Most days I end up doing a lot more than this but the 30-minute mark is a minimum.

Things I like to do for exercise:
- Morning walks or runs.
- Participate in sports like jiu jitsu or softball.
- Lift weights.

Exercising has many benefits. According to the CDC, "Only a few lifestyle choices have as large an impact on your health as physical activity. People who are physically active for about 150 minutes a week have a 33% lower risk of all-cause mortality than those who are physically inactive" ("Physical Activity" 2022).

Known physical benefits of exercise:
- Lower blood pressure
- A healthier heart
- A more attractive physique
- Strengthens your bones and muscles
- Improves your ability to do daily activities and prevent falls
- Increase your chances of living longer
- Reduces your risk of: cardiovascular disease, Type 2 Diabetes and Metabolic Syndrome, and some cancers (bladder, breast, colon, endometrium, esophagus,

kidney, lung, and stomach)

Not only are there a lot of physical benefits of exercise, but there are also mental benefits as well. A study shows that our mental health and firepower are directly linked to our physical fitness regimen (Hogan et al. 2013).

Known mental benefits of exercise:
- Improved concentration
- Sharper memory
- Faster learning
- Prolonged mental stamina
- Enhanced creativity
- Lower stress
- Elevated mood

A study done at Leeds Beckett University evaluated the influence of daytime exercise among office workers with access to a company gym. The study found that on days when the employees went to the gym, their work experience changed. They reported that they could manage their time better, be more productive, and have better interactions with their co-workers. The study also showed that when the workers went home for the day, they felt more satisfied after working out during the day (Coulson et al. 2008).

It is simple: Exercise makes us better workers. If you exercise daily, you will remember more information, work more efficiently, and be more productive in your work. Stop making excuses and start exercising. Recognize exercise is important on your journey to financial freedom.

Four Exercise Tips:
- Find something you enjoy
- Find a workout buddy or join a group
- Invest in your fitness
- Create small habit

Examples of Small Habits:

Every day when you wake up, go on a 30-minute walk. You will get sun exposure early in the day, plus all the mental and physical benefits of exercise. Also, if you go on a walk with a buddy, you will enhance your social health.

Get some at-home videos or find some for free on the internet. Try and do a 30-minute workout five times a week. Set a schedule and stick to it.

Get on a lifting routine where you will lift weights 3-5 days a week. Go to the gym at the same time and on the same days each week, so you do not even need to think about it.

Join group classes that meet regularly.

Join a sports team that plays every week. You can join adult softball, basketball, jiu jitsu, volleyball, or any activity you want.

Go on hikes around where you live. Set a day to go and do a hike on a weekly basis.

Self-Care

How I make sure I am physically healthy:

Taking care of yourself seems silly to talk about but it is so important to your overall physical health. I know myself better than anyone and I try and be an advocate for my own health.

How I practice self-care:

- Daily showers
- Brush my teeth at least twice a day
- Take daily multi vitamins
- Visit the doctor when necessary

Wellness Check-Ups

Physical health also involves keeping up on your wellness. Getting yearly checkups is always a good practice. Make sure to have a general doctor you can go to. They will know your health history, treat you better, and recognize potential problems faster.

Be an advocate for your health. Even though your doctor tells you to take a medicine, you should still research it. Never put anything into your body that you do not know about. Try to understand if it is a medicine that you NEED or medicine that may help you and this is a question you can ask your doctor.

Avoiding alcohol and drugs

Drug and alcohol abuse has a direct impact on not only your health but also your success. According to the CDC these four areas are affected by drug and alcohol use:

• Premature death, chronic health issues, and increased medical costs

• Increased risk for workplace injuries, accidents, and non-work injuries

• Increased rates of absence and overuse of sick and paid leave time

• Loss of productivity, impaired performance, and lower quality of work

("Alcohol and Substance Misuse" 2020)

These side effects of drug use can cause an array of problems to someone's health and how they work. To be successful, you must be productive, have a good quality of work, and make good decisions, but these are impacted by drug and alcohol abuse.

Alcohol and drug use statistics (OPM n.d.)

• Approximately 1 in every 11 workers in the US (9% of the total workforce) struggled with a substance or alcohol use disorder in the past 12 months.

• Alcohol use problems cost US companies between 33-68 billion dollars each year in increased insurance, healthcare, and lowered productivity and attendance costs.

• Drug and alcohol abuse in the workplace accounts for 65% of on-the-job accidents, and that 38% to 50% of all workers' compensation claims are related to the abuse of alcohol or drugs in the workplace.

Remember, you only get one body, so do not mess it up.

Take your physical health seriously, and it will directly correlate with more success in life. Build habits that will help you maintain good physical health and try and stay away or limit things that will be detrimental to your physical health. It is that simple.

Now that we are at the end of Section 2, I want you to list three small steps you can take to better each section of health.

Social health:

1.

2.

3.

Mental health:

1.

2.

3.

Physical health:

1.

2.

3.

SECTION 3: GAIN KNOWLEDGE

Principle 3: Gain Knowledge. You must have knowledge about your work, business interest, and skills to be successful. You also should always strive to learn more as you obtain new information that will help you on your journey.

CHAPTER 7: GET SCHOOLED

There are no secrets to success. It is the result of preparation, hard work, and learning from failure.

— Colin Powell, US statesman and retired four-star General in the United States Army

K nowledge is powerful. It helps keep us safe, and guides us as we navigate life. Whether you grew up in a household that valued education or not, you were learning. We are hard-wired to absorb and use knowledge, right from the start.

When I entered my freshmen year of high school, I started to realize the importance and value of an education. I always made sure my grades were good, and I was constantly trying to learn. My dream was to get a softball scholarship to pay for my college, but I knew that in order to do that, I had to be great at both softball and school. I was able to get a softball scholarship and got my college education paid for.

I went to college and double majored in two different degrees to try and set myself up for as many work avenues as possible. I knew that I wanted to be a high school health teacher, but I also wanted a backup plan.

After getting my bachelor's degree, I got my dream job. A high school teacher and a head softball coach. I then decided to get my master's degree. I looked at all the different options for my master's degree but I decided to go with an online program.

I had gone to college, went to graduate school, and became a teacher but now there was something else I wanted to become knowledgeable about:

Real Estate.

As I was flipping that first house I was constantly in "schooling" mode. I was learning how to do construction from different people, YouTube, and many different online websites. I learned as I was on the journey and I put my head down and just did the work. I was always open to someone's help and willing to learn, both attributes that helped me along my journey to financial freedom.

To this day in my journey, I still use the construction knowledge that I gained in my first house. Having the knowledge of construction has really helped me in finding and fixing those deals no one else wants.

Don't think of schooling as just high school and college; schooling can be anywhere where you learn. In this case, the first house I fixed up was the school and I was the student.

In the next section, I'm going to talk about how you can maximize your various academic journeys through high school, college, and beyond. If you are already through high school or college, you may just skip over discussions about that level.

High School

High school is a kid's first opportunity to specialize in what they want to learn. Of course, you still have to take the core classes, but you are able to take other classes that you enjoy as well.

In high school, however, it is crucial to be a kid. I know it is easy to want to get a job or try and start your journey to success when you are in high school. However, I urge you to do the opposite. Take advantage of the knowledge you will gain in high school but do not grow up too fast. You can do small projects, internships, or even work part-time to save some money, but try not to go overboard. Hang out with your friends, go to dances, and be a kid while you still can.

Be involved in your high school as much as possible. High school has so many different clubs, sports, and activities. If you are interested in something, high school would be an excellent time to join a club and be around others who have the same interests. Not only will you learn more about what you love in those clubs, but also you will create lifelong friendships.

Lastly, take advantage of high school. Yes, public

education has its flaws, but there are many good things that can come out of it. When you're in class, do your best to listen and get as smart as you can in those few years.

I firmly believe that if anyone takes advantage of high school and gets a good foundation of knowledge, they can start their journey to success right out of high school.

College

Degree vs. Knowledge

Before you go to college and get into loads of student loan debt, you need to figure out if college is right for you. First, ask yourself, do you need a degree or just knowledge? If you need a degree for what you want to be when you grow up, college is necessary. If you just need some knowledge in a particular area, you may just go and take a few classes that suit your passion.

You do not need to do all of the college classes if it is not necessary for you. Just take a class or two that fits your needs or find resources online. For example, Stanford puts all of its college lectures online for free. If knowledge is what you need, that may be an excellent place to start.

Benefits of College

There are many benefits of college. I went to college. I knew that I wanted to be a high school teacher and to do that, I needed a degree. If you go to college just to have fun and do not pay attention in your classes, it is a waste of your time and money. The experience of college is also a great benefit. You will meet a lot of cool people and have a lot of fun. I still keep in contact with friends from college, and even some of my professors.

College also provides you with an easy way to move from home. You may have to take out some student loans, but if you need to move out of your house, then college will give you reasonable student housing, and you will be able to live on campus.

Lastly, there are a lot of scholarship options to pay for school. If you can get all of your school paid for, I see no reason why you shouldn't go to college. Look into different scholarships the school offers and make sure to apply for FAFSA (Federal Student Aid). If money is not an issue, go to college and soak up as much information as possible. If money is an issue, then try and decide if you need a degree or just knowledge.

Disadvantages of College

College also comes with its disadvantages. Two disadvantages are money and time. College costs a lot of money and takes a lot of time, and you may find yourself in a heap of student loan debt at the end of college. If you are taking out student loans, you need to stop, take a step back and figure out if the loans are worth it for your degree.

3 Tips When Going To College

1. Decide what you want to do before you go to college: If you decide that college is right for you, know what you want to be before you go. If you have a good understanding of what you want to be, getting your degree will be faster and less expensive.

2. Set yourself up for multiple job options: When in college, you should try and set yourself up for multiple degrees. Even if you cannot double major or pick up a second minor, it is always good to take a class you feel might benefit you. For example, I double-majored in "Health and Physical Education" and "Health and Human Performance" but then took a couple of classes on business because I knew I wanted to start a business one day.

3. Keep your options open to fully set yourself up for success when thinking about college. Throughout your life, you may want to change your job or path, and it is a good idea to give yourself those options starting in college.

Do I need college?

Do this exercise to try and decide if college is right for you.

What are three jobs I would like to do?

Do they need a degree or any school? If so, What type?

How much will a degree or schooling cost? (Skip this if you do not need schooling)

What will my salary be?

Is the degree worth getting for this job?

Other School Options

Luckily, going to college is not the only option. Online schools or trade schools are also great options. You also may just learn from life experiences or by completing an internship. It is essential to know and understand all your options before doing something that can impact the rest of your life.

Online schools

Online schools are a great option if money is stopping you from going to college. If you just need a degree for your dream job, an online school will get you that degree at a fraction of the price. You can stay living at home or live anywhere while going to school. Online school also frees up a lot of time to have a full-time job or participate in an internship of some sort while getting your degree.

Online schooling is a great option to keep in mind when thinking about college. I went to college and lived on campus for my bachelor's degree, and then I completed my master's degree at an online school. I learned just as much with the online degree, and it was a lot more convenient and affordable for me at the time. I was a teacher, flipped my first house, trained for an MMA fight, and got my master's degree—all at the same time.

Trade schools

Trade schools are a great option. If you want to do a specific trade, I suggest looking into trade school instead of college. Here is a list of the 15 highest paying trades you can get a degree in at a trade school:

15 highest paying trades: (Gillis 2022)

1. Plumber
2. Construction Manager
3. Elevator Mechanic
4. Electrical Powerline Technician
5. Aircraft Mechanic
6. Geological and Petroleum Technician
7. Boilermaker
8. Electrician
9. HVAC Technician
10. Rotary Drill Operator
11. Home and Building Inspector
12. Landscape Architect
13. Wind Turbine Technician
14. Solar Photovoltaic Installer
15. Millwright

Internships

Try and find an internship that is paid so you can at least get some money for your time. However, if you do not need the paycheck and the internship seems like you could learn a lot from it, then go and do it. Internships provide you with hands-on experience, and you can see if the job is what you want to do. Internships are also a great way to form good connections, and a lot of times, they will offer you a job if you do well throughout internship.

Learning by doing

Learning by doing is the type of schooling I did when I flipped my first house. I had never done it before but I figured it out. Like I said earlier, the house was the school and I was the student. Sometimes you can learn as much just by doing. Make sure to get as much knowledge as possible and find someone to show you the ropes but the best way to learn is by doing. If you choose this option, you get thrown out into life, and you either sink or swim. If you are smart, find good resources, and have a good work ethic, you will swim.

There are many different schooling options and everyone's situation is different. Make sure the schooling option you pick is right for you and your situation. Before spending a lot of money on school make sure it is going to be worth it.

What are two types of schooling you are interested in?

1.

2.

CHAPTER 8: LEARN FROM RESOURCES

The more that you read, the more things you will know. The more that you learn, the more places you'll go.

– Dr. Seuss

After I graduated from "the school of flipping my first house" there was still much more to learn. Every day on my way to and from work, I would listen to podcasts on real estate, health, passive income, you name it. I made it a goal to spend every extra minute learning. When I was relaxing in my newly remodeled basement apartment, I would watch YouTube videos and read forums. I was always trying to absorb as much knowledge as I could.

One day after a long day of work, I was watching a video on house hacking. Essentially you start how I had started. You buy a house with 5% down as your primary residence and you move into it. Once that house is stabilized and making you some income then buy your next house as your primary residence with 5% down and rent out your old one.

Then it hit me... I need to buy another property! I am sitting here wasting all this time relaxing in my newly remodeled home when I should be expanding my portfolio!

I went back to my first goal to save money each month now that renovations were not eating up my teacher's income. I made it a goal to save at least $2,500 a month. I was able to save an extra $500 now because I did not have to pay rent and I had an extra $200 in rental income.

My Monthly Budget:

Income: $3,200
Teacher Income: $3,000
Cashflow 1st House: $200

Expenses: $700
Food: $200
Gas: $200
Gym: $100
Other: $200

Total Monthly Savings: $2,500

Finally, four months later, I had saved up $10,000, and just at that time I ran across my next property. At this point, I was becoming very knowledgeable about real estate. From all the research I had done, I knew that I had put myself in a position to buy another home as my primary residence.

I ran a search for multi-family homes that had been on the market for a while. There it was. A duplex for $150,000. The property had been on the market for over a year and no one wanted to buy it because the property needed a new roof and had a lot of plumbing issues.

However, that did not scare me, I knew I could do it. I immediately ran the numbers like I had learned to do and walked the property and I knew I wanted this duplex. I put in an offer and had a local roofer go look and give me a roof quote.

The roof was going to be $10,000 and the down payment was going to be $7,750. I was $7,750 short. I did more research and after learning as much as I could, I came up with this plan:

1. Buy the property.
2. The day after closing open up a credit card that is interest free for the first year with a $10,000 limit.
3. Get all the major repairs done in the first two weeks and put it all on the card.
4. Rent out the two units in the property in the first month to cashflow $800 a month and with me still living for free save $3,500 a month.
5. Pay off the credit card within four months

I had a plan, I followed the plan, and I had the credit card paid off within four months of purchasing the property, with an additional $800 monthly income from this duplex. After the card had been paid off, I now was able to save $3,300 a month.

My Monthly Budget:

Income: $4,000
Teacher Income: $3,000
Cashflow 1st Property: $200
Cashflow 2nd Property: $800

Expenses: $700
Food: $200
Gas: $200
Gym: $100
Other: $200

Total Monthly Savings: $3,300

Resources

In today's day and age, anyone can access knowledge. Most everyone has a smartphone sitting in their pocket, giving everyone the key to learning. Today's technology is a gift, but as we all know, it can also be a curse. How you use different resources is up to you. You can get a college education just by using your phone if you do so correctly.

To learn anything, you must be willing to put in the time to learn. You can do this in your free time, on long drives, or even while you are on a walk or a run. Try and find time in the day to learn.

Understand the difference between good information and bad information. Never just hear or read something and believe it. Make sure it is coming from a quality source, and be a critic of the information you are learning.

Look at who is sharing this information. What are their qualifications? Where are they getting their information from? Is the information fact-based or opinion-based? Lastly, always form your own opinions about what you learn.

Books

Books are a great source of knowledge, which are often forgotten about by the younger generation. Books have been around forever, but now you can have an infinite number of books on your devices. To be honest, I was not a big reader in high school or college; I hated it. However, now when I read books, I have found a love for reading because I read books that apply to my life.

Books are excellent because they provide you with an opportunity to learn from someone else directly. People write books about things they are incredibly knowledgeable about, and those books are a sneak peek into their brain. You can find books on pretty much anything. Whatever you are interested in or whatever you want to learn about.

Here is a list of great books to read:

1. *Rich Dad Poor Dad* by Robert Kiyosaki
2. *The Book on Rental Property Investing* by Brandon

Turner

3. *Building Wealth One House at a Time* by John Schaub

4. *The Gift* by Edith Edgar

5. *Man's Search for Meaning* by Viktor Frankl

Podcasts

Just like books, podcasts make it so anyone can share their knowledge. You have to be a little more critical about podcasts because they tend to be very opinion-based. Also, many people have podcasts, and some people shouldn't be teaching anyone, so be aware of whom you are listening to. Always make sure to form your ideas and opinions, and just because someone you might look up to has a particular opinion does not mean you have to.

There are podcasts on all different subjects, and I love listening to podcasts. Podcasts are a great choice when I drive long distances, go on a walk, or just need some background noise.

Here is a list of great podcasts:

1. "On the Market" by Bigger Pockets

2. "Tax Smart Real Estate Investor Podcast"

3. "The Tim Ferriss Podcast"

4. "The Habit Coach" with Ashdin Doctor

5. "Optimal Living Daily"

6. "Break Free Real Estate" with Jocelyn Kaufman

Quick Note!

I am the co-host of a real estate podcast called "Break Free Real Estate". The podcast is for new real estate investors looking to create passive income with real estate. You can learn more about the podcast here: www.joceyj.com/podcast-breakfree

Online Videos And Websites

Videos and websites are also a great way to learn. You can watch YouTube videos on just about anything. Most companies will put out free information to the public. When you are searching, make sure you are finding credible information. Form your own opinion and always be a critic of what you read and learn on the internet.

For the use of websites, use these steps to determine if it is a piece of credible information:

1. Who is the author?
2. Is the site current?
3. Does the story match the headline?
4. Where are they getting their information?
5. Who is the site for?
6. Do not be afraid to ask questions.

People

Everyone is knowledgeable about something. I firmly believe that you can learn something from everyone. If you truly want to be knowledgeable, you should openly listen to what everyone has to say. You can learn from those around you, like your teachers, family, friends, bosses, colleagues, etc. Ask questions as much as you can and try to absorb as much information as you can. If you find out someone you know is very knowledgeable about something, buy them lunch and pick their brain.

We live in a world where knowledge is at the tip of our fingers. Take advantage and start to learn more and more. Once you find what you are interested in, that may be the job path you venture down.

I had zero knowledge about real estate four years ago, and now I would consider myself an expert. Not only have I allowed myself to gain all of this knowledge but it has also helped me create financial freedom and a life I love.

Use Your Resources!

List 1 thing you want to be more knowledgeable about:

List 3 different resources you can use to gain knowledge about that subject:

Example: a certain podcast, YouTube channel, book, website, or person.

a.

b.

c.

What resources are you going to use today?

Take action! Choose one of your resource options and make it a goal to start learning about that subject today!

SECTION 4: MONEY MANAGMENT

Principle 4: Money Management. You must be able to make money, save money, budget money, and build a good credit score to become financially free.

CHAPTER 9: UNDERSTANDING WEALTH

A year from now you may wish you had started today.

— Karen Lamb, author

I had worked thus far very hard to get to where I was. I now owned two houses and had a positive net income of $1,000 off of the properties, plus I was living for free. At this point, I was able to save $3,300 a month, but to advance further in real estate I needed to have wealth. I was at a point where I either had to move again and buy another single-family residence after waiting at least 1 year or I had to come up with a 25% down payment. I needed to either wait for a year or acquire enough wealth for a 25% down payment on my next investment.

After researching my different options, I realized I had a lot of equity in both of the properties I currently had. I figured I could potentially tap into this equity and use that for a down payment on my next house. First, I looked into doing a cash-out refinance on the first property I bought. I talked with a few lenders but at that time most lenders were not doing cash-out refinances and so that option did not work, so I ultimately decided to sell my first house. At this time, I also had started getting my realtor's license so I felt I could sell my house without an agent and save the commission fee.

I originally bought my first house for $225,000 and sold it for $324,000 making a profit from the sale of $117,000. Now I had created some wealth; I had $117,000 in the bank to buy another property with. In order to avoid taxes, I decided to do a 1031 exchange so I could put all of the profit from the sale toward my next property. (A 1031 exchange allows you to defer the taxes when you buy another property with the profits from a property you are selling).

In order to make the sale of the property worthwhile, I had to find another property that would make me more money than the property I was selling. After looking at a lot of different properties, I found the perfect one. The property was a 10-plex for $397,000. Only two of the units were rented at $600 each and the other units had been vacant for a while and needed a lot of work. After successfully purchasing the property, I moved there to start the remodeling process. Thankfully, my cousin, came as well to help me get the place up and running.

Within two months I had all the units repaired and rented out. The 10 plex was now netting $4,500 a month and increased my monthly savings even more! Because

I sold the place I was living, I moved back in with my mom and started paying $500 in rent again but now my monthly savings moved up to $7,100.

My Monthly Budget:

Income: $8,300
Teacher Income: $3,000
Cashflow 2nd Property: $800
Cashflow 3rd Property: $4,500

Expenses: $1,200
Rent: $500
Food: $200
Gas: $200
Gym: $100
Other: $200

Total Monthly Savings: $7,100

Why Is Wealth Important

Wealth is the total amount of money and/or assets you have. Wealth in America today includes the USD (today's US dollar), bitcoin (or other cryptocurrencies), equity in stocks, real estate, and anything else that holds value.

Wealth is the driving force of our economy. You cannot buy something if you do not have money. You cannot pay rent or pay a mortgage if you do not have money. You NEED money to live. I always hear the saying, "money doesn't make you happier." However, a certain amount of money can improve your quality of life. A study in 2018 from Purdue University found different income points. The study found that the ideal salary for emotional well-being is $75,000 for individuals because it will cover the costs of living and provide some stability. Next, the study found that the ideal salary for life satisfaction is $95,000 for individuals. (Jebb et al 2018). An additional twenty thousand dollars can make a huge difference in how satisfied you are with your life.

Living paycheck to paycheck is stressful, and taking a job you do not want, just to put food on the table, sucks. This is why you need to set yourself up NOW. I genuinely believe that all of you reading this book CAN become financially free if you set your mind to do so. If you want to be free with your time and do not want to do a job that you hate, you need money.

Steps to Wealth

1. Make money.

2. Manage your money.

3. Save as much money as possible to prepare for Section 5: Creating Passive Income.

CHAPTER 10: MAKE MONEY

Too many people spend money they earned, to buy things they don't want, to impress people that they don't like.

-Will Rogers

After I got my real estate license, I decided to sell the second property I bought. I originally bought the property for $150,000, and it sold for $300,000, so with some fees I had a total profit from the sale of $147,000. I sold this house 9 months after buying it meaning I made $147,000 in 9 months! I did not do a 1031 exchange on this property to avoid all the hoops I would have had to jump through and I ended up having to pay $35,000 in taxes due to the capital gains I received. I still made $112,000 on this property in 9 months but if I could go back, I would have held the property for at least 1 year (to lessen the taxes paid) or used another 1031 exchange.

Regardless, I made $112,000.

Next, 8 months after I bought my third property (the 10-plex) I had created a lot of equity. I wanted to buy more properties so I needed more than just $112,000 from my last house sale. I decided to do a cash-out refinance on my 10-plex and the property appraised at $910,000! When I bought it 8 months earlier for $397,000!

This was a huge turning point in my journey and gave me a turbo boost on my journey to financial freedom. I was able to tap into the property and access 75% of the equity the property had, so with the cash-out refinance, I was able to access $350,000!

Now between the house I sold and the cash-out refinance of my 10-plex, I had made $462,000 to invest to create more income. Due to selling my second property, my monthly income had decreased $800, and due to the mortgage increase from the cash-out refinance on my 10-plex, my income had decreased by $1,000. I was confident I could make up the $1,800 difference plus more income with my new investments. I saw this as a small step backwards that was going to prepare me for a huge leap forward.

My Monthly Budget:

Income: $6,500
Teacher Income: $3,000
Cashflow 3rd Property: $3,500

Expenses: $1,200
Rent: $500
Food: $200
Gas: $200
Gym: $100
Other: $200

Total Monthly Savings: $5,300

Now that I had made some serious money, I could buy some more properties and increase my income even more. Next, I bought a 4-plex for $167,000 that needed some work. I bought the property, hired out the work to a local contractor and then rented out the property for a monthly cashflow of $1,000. Then I came across one of the best opportunities of my journey. My realtor in the area found me an insanely amazing off-market deal. It was a 16-unit apartment complex with a huge commercial space making it a 17-plex. The seller wanted $1,000,000 for the property but was willing to do a seller financing deal on it. We had a seller financing deal written up by a lawyer, and we agreed to a 20% down on a 20-year note with a fixed rate of 4% interest. This deal was finalized in January of 2021. If you know anything about real estate you may know how amazing of a deal this was. This property gave me a cash flow of $5,500 a month.

My spouse and I then decided to buy a house together and we each spent $10,000 on the down payment and my personal living expenses increased to $1,250 a month. I was now making enough money monthly and I decided to retire from teaching and focus all my efforts on building my monthly passive income.

I had now spent $262,000 of the money I made off my other properties and still had $200,000 to invest.

My Monthly Budget:

Income: $10,000
Cashflow 3rd Property: $3,500
Cashflow 4th Property: $1,000
Cashflow 5th Property: $5,500

Expenses: $1,950
Mortgage: $1,250
Food: $200
Gas: $200
Gym: $100
Other: $200

Total Monthly Savings: $8,050

Since I was no longer teaching, I was able to focus all my efforts on real estate. I started focusing more on being a realtor for other investors and providing them with a great experience when buying an investment property. I have successfully helped dozens of people get started in investing and creating passive income. Being a realtor also provides me with more income that solely goes into savings that can be used for creating more passive income. I get to decide when I work, where I work, and whom I help. I do not depend on the income I receive as a real estate agent, so I am able to give my clients a unique experience. I have turned down real estate clients because they were not nice or honest people and because I have created passive income, I have the freedom to do so.

Hearing about my success may be very inspiring and at the same time seem impossible but it is essential to remember you have to start somewhere. I would have gotten nowhere in my journey to financial freedom if I never had a job to make money in the first place. In order to invest you need to have money. Initially, I wanted to be a teacher and I figured being a teacher would provide stable income and plus I could get all of the weekends and holidays off. However, it was clear to me early on that I wanted to create wealth, and that wasn't going to happen being a teacher for the rest of my life.

I have nothing against the profession, and I admire those who choose it. Still to this day I love teaching— the teacher in me comes through in this book, as I am essentially teaching you. I enjoyed my job as a teacher and so it was a great job for me to save money. Even if I were still a teacher today and I never went down the real estate rabbit hole, I would be happy and content because I truly loved my job and I had great benefits.

Work is something everyone has to do to some degree.

You have to work. Working is simply trading your time for money. How much money your time is worth is how much you get paid. Growing up there is so much pressure on what you want to do for work. Some people have a good idea of what they want to do, and others have literally no idea. Trust me, either way, it is OK. Your goal should be to obtain multiple skills so you can have different job options.

Also, keep in mind you do not have to have the same job for your whole life. Never be dependent on one line of work because our world is constantly changing, and you do not want to be left without a way to make money.

How To Decide What To Do For Work

When trying to figure out what you want to do for work, find a job you enjoy. If you enjoy numbers and math, find a job that includes those skills. If you enjoy computers, find a job that has to do with computers. Never just go into a line of work because you think it will make a lot of money. Money should be a factor, but how much you enjoy that job is also an important factor.

When looking at a job, ask yourself if you would enjoy it. Will you enjoy the task, your boss, and your co-workers? Next, ask yourself if the amount of money you are making per hour is worth it. If you are making a ton of money, maybe you will give up a little enjoyment. On the other hand, if you love your job, perhaps you are willing to take a little bit less of a paycheck. The sweet spot is finding a job that you love, and that pays well. If you can do that, then you have hit a gold mine.

In today's world, it is also very possible to find a side job that will allow you to save even more money. You can even drive Uber or deliver Door Dash in your spare time. There are many options like these where you can create your hours and have even more money to put into your savings account.

Find A Job You Will Love

What are some things you enjoy doing?

1.

2.

3.

What is one line of work for each of your loves?

1.

2.

3.

What is the pay for each of these jobs?

1.

2.

3.

Which job will you enjoy the most but will provide you with enough income to be able to save money?

Military

The military is an excellent choice out of high school. If you are unsure what you want to do or have a passion for joining, the military provides a great path to success. The cool thing about the military is that you can stay in the military for an entire career or just join for the standard four years of active duty and four years of non-active duty. Additionally, the military is a good option if you do not have a lot of money or are unsure what to do; the military can set you up for success. You can work in the military and get a monthly paycheck, but also your living expenses will be paid for, which will allow you to save a lot more money. The military also provides a lot of great benefits like health insurance, retirement, great loan options, and free college. If you want to get a degree in something, you can join the military and get it for free. You can get your degree while in the military or wait until you are out of the military to go to college. The military is also an excellent option because you can start investing and creating passive income while you are still in the military. In the four years it takes someone to get a degree, you could already be generating thousands of dollars each month in passive income.

The military may be a good option, and you should see and understand why the military can set you up for success. However, you must realize it is a commitment, and it is a job. When you join the military most of the time you cannot quit. The military will hold you to a higher standard, and you will be told what to do while you are in the military. You may have to go to war and you are signing your life over to the military while you are enlisted. You must research this path and ensure it is something you want to do before you sign up. Understand the pros and cons and if the military is a good path for you.

Family

Another way you may be able to make money is from your family. You may receive money from your family, whether it be a lot, a little, or none. My advice is to save this money. It is easy to blow money given to you, but you should try and save all of it for the future. If you are lucky and receive a large amount of money for one reason or another, you must be smart with the money and not blow it. Still, find a job and a good path in life, and then once you have that settled, keep saving money, and then you will be ready for Section 5 and can invest.

Making Money

After I was able to create some more passive income and decide when and where I worked, the quality of my life increased. Don't get me wrong I did have a lot of freedom as a teacher but now I am able to travel whenever I want and spend my time how I want to. I get to spend more time with family and friends and I have more freedom throughout my day to do things I enjoy doing.

To live on this earth, let alone be successful, you must make money. Whether you get money from your family, earn money at work, or save up a bunch of money in the military, you have to find a way to make money. The end goal is to create passive income but first you have to make money to invest.

When you choose a path to go down for work, make sure you enjoy the job and that the job is worth your paycheck. Keep your options open and always try to pick up new skills, that way you are not dependent on one job.

Once you have a way to make money, you will need to save and manage that money.

CHAPTER 11: MONEY MANAGEMENT

Beware of little expenses; a small leak will sink a great ship.

—*Benjamin Franklin*

After I cash out refinanced my 10-plex, bought a 4-plex, and bought the insanely amazing 17-plex deal I was able to save a total of $8,050 each month. I still had $200,000 still to spend on real estate to grow my passive income even more.

I then came across a newly remodeled 4-plex. The 4-plex consisted of two buildings and each building has two units. I bought the 4-plex for $350,000 and it cashflows $1,000 a month. Soon after I also bought a 3-plex for $150,000 that has a monthly cashflow of $1,000 a month. I bought both of these properties with 25% down, leaving me with $75,000 left in my savings.

My Monthly Budget:

Income: $12,000
Cashflow 3rd Property: $3,500
Cashflow 4th Property: $1,000
Cashflow 5th Property: $5,500
Cashflow 6th Property: $1,000
Cashflow 7th Property: $1,000

Expenses: $1,950
Mortgage: $1,250
Food: $200
Gas: $200
Gym: $100
Other: $200

Total Monthly Savings: $10,050

$75,000 is not a huge cushion for the 5 properties I currently own so I am continually focused on money management to try and build my savings back up as much as possible. I want to create a good number of reserves, buy another property, and invest in different passive income strategies. I now personally have over 1 million in equity. I could access that capital to buy more properties but I have decided to work on growing my savings and keep all the equity I have.

To save the maximum amount of money each month and track my progress I have created a few systems to help me.

Monthly Systems

1. At the end of each month, I make sure all payments are made and all expenses are tracked for each property.

2. I put 10% of the gross rental income for each property into a savings account for that property. This savings is for upcoming capital expenditures or emergencies (big expenses the property will have down the road).

3. Transfer the net income from each property into my savings account.

4. Calculate income for the month, expenses, and how much total money I currently have in my bank accounts. I import all of the data into my five-year plan spreadsheet.

5. Analyze the five-year plan spreadsheet and make sure no money is missing and get a good grasp of where I am at financially and what I need to do next.

Yearly systems:

1. At the end of each year, I finalize the five-year plan spreadsheet for that year and track where I am at.

2. I finalize all property books and get them ready to send to my CPA.

3. I get all my books ready for the next year and create a few financial goals.

Money management is one of the most important things in creating passive income. Even if you create a lot of wealth, if you do not manage that money properly it will not last long. Plus if you never are able to manage your money you will likely never save enough money to get started in the passive income strategies in the first place.

If I would have never saved money when I was on my teaching salary, I would have never been able to venture down the path of creating a financially free life. When I started my teaching career and had a steady paycheck coming in each month, I knew I needed to manage my money. As I told you earlier in the book, I first started by writing down my monthly income. Then I wrote down all of my expenses and created a budget for each expense. Next, I subtracted my budget from my income and I put that amount into savings each month as soon as my paycheck hit the bank. As I started investing and creating more income, I was able to put more into savings each month.

Money management is essential to success because if you cannot manage your money, you will never be able to be financially successful. Good money management is crucial to saving money, investing, and being financially free. Money management takes discipline, and not everyone is willing to have good money management. If you want to be successful, you MUST learn to manage your money and save as much as possible to get ready for Section 5: Creating Passive Income.

Tracking

First, you must know where you are spending your money. I want you to go through your last two months of spending. If you are not sure about some expenses, it is okay to guess. Look back through your bank statements to see what you have spent money on. I have a worksheet in this book but I have also included the worksheet and a spreadsheet for money management in the Tools Packet. On the next few pages, I want you to write down what you have spent for the last two months.

Month 1:
Food Total:
Restaurants:

Groceries:

Fast food:

Bills Total:
Rent/mortgage:

Escrow (home insurance & property taxes):

Phone bill:

Gym membership:

Student Loans:

Other bills:

Auto Total:
Auto Payment:

Gas:

Car repairs:

Auto Loans:

Car Insurance:

Health Total:
Doctor visits:

Medicine:

Supplements (Vitamins)

Health insurance (If not covered by employer):

Child support:

Essential Items Total:

Toiletries:

Cleaning supplies:

Work supplies:

Other:

Non-essential items Total:

Shopping:

Events:

Travel:

Entertainment:

Other:

Total essential expenses:

Total non-essential expenses:

Total expenses for the month:

Month 2:

Food Total:

Restaurants:

Groceries:

Fast food:

Bills Total:

Rent/mortgage:

Escrow (home insurance & property taxes):

Phone bill:

Gym membership:

Student Loans:

Other bills:

Auto Total:

Auto Payment:

Gas:

Car repairs:

Auto Loans:

Car Insurance:

Health Total:

Doctor visits:

Medicine:

Supplements (Vitamins)

Health insurance (If not covered by employer):

Child support:

Essential Items Total:

Toiletries:

Cleaning supplies:

Work supplies:

Other:

Non-essential items Total:

Shopping:

Events:

Travel:

Entertainment:

Other:

Total essential expenses:

Total non-essential expenses:

Total expenses for the month:

Budget

Now that you have tracked where you spend your money, it is time to budget to save more money each month. The goal when first starting out on your journey is to live as minimally as possible to save as much money as you can for Section 5: Creating Passive Income.

Have you ever heard the saying that "it takes money to make money?" Well, it is true. To get started in your money-making adventures, you must first save money. As you begin to make more money, it is easy to start spending more, but I urge you to keep saving and investing in your future.

In order to create a budget you can stick to, you must determine what is essential and what is not necessary. For example, if you can live with your parents for free or have a roommate and save a lot of money, that is a way better option than paying the total rent or mortgage by yourself. Always try and think of different ways you can save some extra money in your situation.

For each category, look at your last two months of

expenses and determine how much money you need to set aside for each category. Under each category, I will also share some savings tips.

Budgeting:

Food Budget: $_____

Include: groceries, restaurants, fast food, etc.

If you meal plan each week, you will save a lot of money.

Only allow yourself to eat out at a restaurant once a week.

Bills Budget: $_____

Include: rent/mortgage, phone bill, gym membership, credit card, student loans, etc.

Are there any bills you can cut out?

Are there any bills that have cheaper options?

Could you get a roommate or find a cheaper place to live?

Could you join someone's phone plan for a cheaper phone bill?

Is your interest rate on your student loans high? Should you try and pay extra on it each month?

Auto Budget: $_____

Include: Auto payment, gas, auto repairs, etc.

Do you have a big car payment? Is this something you NEED?

Make sure to budget for gas you may need.

Health Budget: $____

Include: health insurance, doctor bills, medicine, supplements, etc.

Only include health insurance if it is not taken out of your paycheck

Decide a budget that works for you for the doctor. If you have $0 medical expenses, then start with $100, allowing you to go to the doctors if needed.

Essential items Budget: $____

Include: Toiletries, cleaning supplies, work supplies, etc.

You need these things in your house or for work, so create a budget for them.

Non-essential items budget: $____

Include: shopping, presents for others, travel, vacations, etc.

Look at how much you have spent in this category in the last two months and determine a budget. Allow yourself some spending money but not too much.

Total monthly budget amount: $_____

Savings

Savings is the most essential aspect of money management. Everything you budget and track is to find out the maximum number you can save each month for future investments.

Off limits saving account tips:

Tip #1

Have two different savings accounts. Have one savings account tied with your checking account and credit card, and then have another savings account that does not have a checking account linked to it. The savings account that is linked to your checking account can be dipped into for emergencies or for other things like if you want to go on a vacation. The other savings account is off-limits savings and can only be used for Section 5: Creating Passive Income. Having a saving account not linked to a checking or credit card makes it easier to force yourself not to touch it, which is why I think this is a tip everyone should use.

Tip #2

After tracking your expenses and income and coming up with a budget, decide how much money you will put into each savings account. I suggest you take the extra money and put 75% into the off-limits savings account and the other 25% into the general savings account. Pick a number and stick to that number. Try and put that amount into savings each month, no matter what.

Tip #3

If you get a bonus or your paycheck rises, then put the extra money into your off-limits savings account. If you have been doing fine without this money, then do not even allow yourself to see it. Put it directly into your savings, and you will be glad you did.

Go back to your budget and find out how much money you should save each month.

Answer the following questions:

Total budget amount: $_____

Total income: $_____

Total savings (Subtract your total budget from your income): $_____

75% of your total savings (goes into your off-limits savings account): $_____

25% of your total savings (goes into your dip-into savings account): $_____

Right after you get your paycheck, move the money into the accounts, so you are not even tempted. If you have an emergency or one of your budgets goes over, you can use your dip-into savings account to cover the difference. Take your off-limits savings account seriously and only use it for Section 5: Creating Passive Income.

Any extra money you make (bonuses or overtime) should be moved immediately into your off-limits savings account because you already are budgeting without the extra money, so why not save it?

Debt

What if you picked up this book too late? What if you already have debt? Maybe you have student loans or credit card debt but it is not too late for you. In your budget under bills set a budget to pay off your debt each month. Stick to this and once your debts are paid off then you can put that extra money you were paying towards your debt to add to your savings each month.

Credit Score

The last thing I want to touch on in this section is your credit score. Your credit score can make or break deals. It is vital to have good credit going into Pillar 5: Creating Passive Income. Having a high credit score gives you access to more loan products and better interest rates. By having better interest rates and different loan options your monthly cost will be less expensive, which will provide you with more cashflow.

Your credit score is grouped into five categories:

1. payment history (35%)
2. amounts owed (30%)
3. length of credit history (15%)
4. new credit (10%)
5. credit mix (10%)

The easiest way to build credit is to have at least one credit card you use and pay off each month. You get many points and rewards by using a credit card, and if you pay it off each month, you will never have to pay interest. Try not to close a credit card because you want to keep the same cards for as long as possible. I suggest starting with one credit card, and once you get the hang of it, get another. You do not need more than 2 credit cards open.

Please be aware that I am telling you to get a credit card to build your credit and not abuse it. Credit card debt is really easy to enter into, and that is not our purpose. When I was 15 my mom cosigned on a credit card with me and taught me how to use the card to build my credit. Then when I was ready to buy my first property, I had a credit history and it was a lot easier for me to get a loan.

Next, you must be sure to never miss a payment. Missing a payment can be very detrimental for years. If you miss a payment for any type of loan, it can hit your credit score hard, so make sure you are on top of it. Set up automatic payments just in case you forget, and pick a day each month to make sure your payments go through.

Lastly, be careful of how many times your credit is pulled. Every time you apply for a loan or a new card, your credit will be pulled, which can also be a hit on your credit. Only have your credit pulled when necessary and let bankers know you want to wait until absolutely necessary to pull your credit.

Concluding Money

This chapter boils down to finding a job or a way to make money, saving as much of it as possible, and building your credit. If you can do those three things, you are on the right track to financial freedom. After you have built your credit and saved up some money, you are ready for Section 5: Creating Passive Income, and that is when the fun begins.

Remember to continue saving money and building your

credit after starting the fifth step towards financial freedom. You will want to continue to keep good money management skills to keep yourself financially open for more opportunities as they come along.

SECTION 5: CREATE PASSIVE INCOME

Principle 5: Create Passive Income. You must create passive income through entrepreneurship, real estate, or investments. Then you will truly have financial freedom.

CHAPTER 12: WORK EASIER

The rich invest in time, the poor invest in money.

—*Warren Buffett*

B efore I bought my first house. I knew my WHY, I lived a healthy life, I gained a lot of knowledge, and I had $12,000 saved up. I was ready for Section 5. As you know, I invested in a mother-in-law that needed a lot of work. I put a lot of work into the property and then rented it out. I had to do the work because I did not have enough money to pay someone else to do the labor. That mother-in-law started out non-passive and then turned more passive once I rented it out. Next, I bought a duplex that needed some work, did the work, and then rented it out. Then I bought a 10-plex, did the work, then rented it out.

At this point in my journey, I experienced the "snowball" effect with my real estate. Soon after getting the 10-plex settled, I was able to buy two 4-plexes, a 17-unit apartment complex, and a 3-plex. My real estate quickly became more passive and due to the success I had thus far in real estate, I became financially free for the first time in my life. Next, I started investing in stocks, creating a few different businesses, and continuing to grow my real estate to 52 units. I wanted to diversify my money as much as I could so I could have many different income streams. After I had a good amount of income coming in each month I put in my resignation for teaching and went full-time into creating my different income streams.

The 5th step is where all of the work begins. By now you should know your WHY, how to live healthily, how to gain knowledge, and hopefully how to save your money.

For the purpose of this book, I have brought you through my journey to financial freedom but it is important to remember I had to complete each of these steps before I even bought my very first property. Now that I have found financial freedom, I still focus on each of these steps to help me to improve my passive income and the quality of my life.

Section 5 is where you will turn the small amount of savings that you have worked so hard for into a large amount of savings. Once you save and create more money, it becomes easier to make even more money. Money starts to have a "snowball" effect after you successfully complete Section 5 just one time.

There are many ways to grow your savings, but we will focus on these three money-making strategies: Entrepreneurship, real estate, and investments. Please remember that each of these strategies could be a full book in themselves, and each chapter will give you a good starting point but it is up to you to do more research on any strategy you chose.

There is still so much more to learn about each of these strategies, but reading through this section of the book will provide you with a good base of knowledge. One of these strategies may interest you more than the other, but the end goal is to have all three strategies making money for you. I suggest you start with one strategy that makes the most sense for you at this point in your life, but it is crucial to understand the ins and outs of each money-making strategy.

Understand that this section is CREATING passive income. Most of the time your passive income strategies will not start off passive until you have the capital to make them passive.

Passive Income: make money with little to no effort.

Non-Passive Income: make money with effort.

Once you have grown your savings, you can diversify your portfolio and invest in other passive money-making strategies and then turn your non-passive strategies into passive strategies. After you start to grow your savings, it is a good idea to continue to keep your job as security so you can keep growing your income. Slowly begin to make your non-passive strategies more passive and invest in more and more passive money-making strategies.

After you have a good flow of passive income, where you can still save a good amount of money each month, you can quit your job and grow your savings full-time. Plus, you'll get to travel and do whatever the heck you want because you will still have a paycheck coming in each month. Isn't that the dream?

Everyone wants to be financially free but most won't complete Sections 1-4 to get to Section 5; others fail in Section 5. Becoming financially free takes a lot of hard work and if you are willing to put in the work and follow the steps you will one day be financially free.

Anyone can create financial freedom. I did it on a teacher's salary in just four years.

Read through all of the money-making strategies thoroughly, and hopefully, you will have all of these money-making strategies earning you passive income one day.

CHAPTER 13: BECOME AN ENTREPRENEUR

You are never too old to set another goal or to dream a new dream.

—C.S. Lewis, British writer

Thinking about new business ideas is one of my favorite things to do. I currently own a softball business, which I mainly use to do private lessons, and a construction business which allows me to do work on my own properties and to help some clients.

I am in the process of creating passive income with a few other entrepreneurship ventures, one of these ventures is writing this book. I wanted to get my story out to a wider audience so I can help even more people learn how to become financially free. Writing this book has been an amazing experience and something I have really enjoyed working on and hopefully once it is done my book will give me some extra passive income. I am also in the process of creating an app to streamline the real estate process. This business is far from complete but hopefully in the next few years I can make a true impact by mixing technology with real estate.

It takes a certain type of person to become successful in life. If you are lazy or constantly content in your current position in life, chances are you will not become financially free unless you change your mindset. I was lucky to have the correct mindset from an early age. I have always dedicated myself fully to whatever I was doing in that moment—whether it be softball, school, real estate, etc. I always kept a can-do attitude and if I ever ran into an obstacle, I pushed through it and never allowed myself to give up.

To be a successful entrepreneur you have to dedicate yourself to that project, and NEVER give up. Anyone can start a business or have a dream, but not everyone will succeed. Everyone dreams of coming up with a great invention that will change the world and make them super-rich. Everyone dreams of starting a business from the ground up and retiring at 30. Everyone dreams of these things, but most people still have their W-2 jobs until they retire at 60. The key is having the right attitude and determination. If you dream of being an entrepreneur, you must work hard because it is not easy, and it will take dedication.

If you are interested in starting your own business, take some time to investigate the many options out there. There are many different forms of entrepreneurship, and each of them has its advantages. Some entrepreneurship ideas are passive, and some are non-passive. Most businesses will start out very non-passive and will require a lot of work to start. Most entrepreneurs have to work a regular W-2 job while starting a business to keep themselves afloat financially.

Don't let money hold you back from pursuing your business. Entrepreneurship is something you can start with $0. Out of all the passive income strategies we will talk about in this book, entrepreneurship is the only one that does not typically require a large sum of money to start. Instead of waiting to create a business until you have a bunch of money saved up, you can potentially skip to this step and use your business as your income stream. While it may be easier to start a business if you do have a nest egg of money, it is possible to start with nothing which makes this strategy a super powerful tool.

How To Start A Business From The Ground Up

1. Identify a problem or need

With any type of business you create, make sure there is a need for your idea. If there is no need you will not have any customers. To identify a problem or need you may start by asking yourself these questions:

- Is there anything in my life that causes a problem?

- What may make my life easier?

- Is there something I feel people really need?

2. Find the solution

To find the solution you must figure out a way to create value for someone with that problem or need. To figure this out you must first talk with different people who have the need and try and identify some solutions. Once you have a few ideas you will want to test those ideas against each other. For example, you can run different experiments such as three different fake Facebook ads to see how many clicks each ad gets. This experiment can give you a good idea of which business idea will be most successful. Other ways to test your ideas are to send out surveys, talk to your friends and family, and research what other solutions are currently out there.

3. Create a business

Pick your name: When picking your name, you should use different testing methods to see what name will perform best. You can create some surveys or ads and see which name will be most effective. It is also important to make sure that the name is available and not being used. You can find out if the name is being used by a simple google search or going to your local state business platform and performing a name search. Picking the right name can make or break your business so take your time on this.

File for an LLC or Corporation: Depending on your state and your business there are different ways to go about filing for your business license. You will want to research your city and state and find the best way to go about setting up your business. You can do some research and set up the LLC or Corporation yourself, hire a lawyer to do it for you, or use an online platform that creates LLC or Corporations. I suggest to chat with a CPA and or Lawyer to confirm you have the right documents and know different tax implications of your business.

Buy the website domain and create a website: Once you pick your name, it's a good idea to go ahead and buy the website domain, even if you don't plan to have a website right away. You can go to sites like GoDaddy or Hover and purchase any available domain that you would like. Once you purchase a domain, you own it forever, so it makes sense to secure that from the beginning. The website domain is important to have if you plan to grow your business. Once you buy the domain create a website for your business. You can learn how to do this yourself or hire a website designer to make you the perfect website.

Create social media profiles: Social media is a great way to grow your business and keep people informed about your business. Even if you are not planning on using social media to grow your business, I suggest you try and secure the usernames for major social media sites, in case you need them down the road.

Start working your A** off: Once you have your business created, it is time to put in the work. No matter what the business is, you will have to put in a lot of hours to make it worth it. You should create a website, social media content, and start to get people interested in your business. Experiment with different ad platforms to see what works. Continue to research and learn. Above all, stay focused and put in the hard work required to make your business a success.

4. Grow your business

Pitch to investors: If you are planning on getting investors for your business, you will want to create a business plan and pitch your business to them. This is not a necessary step for all businesses but can help expedite the process.

Promote your business: Tell all of your family and friends about your business and ask them to share with their friends. See if you can get some free exposure from people around you.

Pay for ads: You can pay for some ads on Facebook or Google to target users that will want to use your business. The ads can direct the customers to your website, social media, or your personal site, if chosen.

Create a referral program: Once you have had some buzz, create some type of incentive for people to share your business. You can offer free or discounted services for referrals.

Adjust your business to meet your clients' needs: As your

business grows and you get more user feedback you will want to adjust as your business. If you continue to adjust and continue to meet the needs of your consumers, your business will be more likely to succeed.

5. Automate your business

The whole point of this book is to break free of the W-2 job and create passive income. Once you start your business, you should look for ways to automate it. Create systems and hire some key employees that can free up your time. However, do not do this too soon. It is important to put in the work first to get your business to a good point, where it is stable before you experiment to much with automation that eats into your monthly income.

Learn More About Different Business Types

Each and every business is different from the other and each different business has different needs. I am simply providing you an outline of how to create and start a business. You need to adjust the outline to the needs of the business you want to start.

There are many different business types today and technology is making many different business opportunities possible. You can create an online service, create a product, open a local business, become a content creator, or invest in one of the high-cost-cash-flowing business ideas. Each type of business is very different from the other and they all require different resources. For the purpose of this book, I am giving you a general idea of each business type. If you want to learn more about a certain business type, you will want to do your own in-depth research.

Online Service

A great example of a successful online service is TurboTax. The creators of TurboTax were able to identify a need literally everyone in America has: how to file your taxes properly but without spending a lot of money for a CPA. A majority of people have simple taxes and can't afford to pay a CPA each year to file their taxes. TurboTax created an online software that files someone's taxes after providing the proper information. Turbo tax is very successful and the reason being they came up with a great solution to meet a need a lot of people have.

In today's world almost anything can be turned into an online service. If you look at companies like Amazon, Netflix, and Airbnb they did not exist 20 years ago. The creators of these online services identified that there was a need and the founders figured out a solution that works.

Creating an online service is a great option because you can start with little to no capital. As long as you have a computer and some basic knowledge of computers, you can get started. There are a ton of free and low cost online courses you can take to acquire the skills that are needed to start an online business.

Skills you need: Basic WordPress skills, know how to use tools like Google Analytics or Mix Panel, Basic web design, photo editing, basic copyrighting skills, social media skills, learn how to run ads, and basic SEO (Search Engine Optimization).

Skills you may need but can hire out: Copyrighting, SEO, Web Design, App design, Programmer, and digital marketing.

As you start your business, you will most likely have to do most of the work. To hire people, you need money and many entrepreneurs are starting with nothing. With some basic skills, you can put together the start of an online service so investors can get a good idea of the possibilities. Then you may be able to start to acquire capital and hire some key employees.

Creating/Inventing A Product:

Casper is a mattress company that is becoming more and more popular. Most of you reading this book have probably seen a Casper ad and some of you probably even have a Casper mattress in your bedroom. Casper did not become one of the leading mattress companies due to the comfort of their bed; instead, they solved a problem people had. Before Casper revolutionized the mattress business, a lot of people had a hard time getting their new bed into their bedroom, picking the bed up from the store, or paying a large amount of money for shipping and handling to get the bed into their room.

Casper recognized this problem and came up with the simple idea of "a bed in a box." Casper took the newly popular idea of a foam mattress and made it easily transferable to homes. They highlighted the simplicity of shipping this brand-new bed directly to your home and the easy transportation possibilities. People like simple things and it's safe to say Casper was a hit. Many other mattress companies have popped up afterward and duplicated the "bed in a box" process and this is a great example of a product that is successful. Mattresses already existed before Casper; they just improved upon the idea. They identified a need and came up with a great solution.

Creating a product is one of the more popular avenues of an entrepreneur. Think about everything you use on a daily basis, and now think about the fact that most of those products were created by a person. Entrepreneurs are always thinking of problems and ways to solve them and that's why most successful entrepreneurs will have ventured in a few different businesses.

With creating a product, you can test the idea and see if it is a solution people will use. One of the best tools you can use is to run a kick starter campaign. You can run a kick starter campaign with just an idea; you don't even need the product. There are so many different options in what you can offer the customers if they support your company. You can offer people first access to your product once it becomes available or even a t-shirt with a donation of a certain amount. Running a kick starter campaign can give you a great idea of how successful your product may be.

After you come up with your idea, you must make the product and figure out the logistics.

- Can you make and produce the product?

- Will you have to outsource the production of your product?

- How much will the product cost to ship?

- How much does the product cost to make?

- How much will you charge for the product?

If you are planning on selling your product online, you will need to create an online presence and a way to sell the product to people using the internet. Once you have all the logistics figured out then you need to decide if you want to bring on investors or partners to fund the deal, or if you want to do it yourself.

Local Business: Restaurant, Store, Car Shop, Lawn Mowing Service, Etc.

I knew a kid in high school who started a local lawn mowing business. In my neighborhood, there were not a lot of yard maintenance companies and the ones that existed were expensive. I lived in the suburbs, so all the houses were close together and walking distance from each other. This boy asked his parents if he could borrow their lawn mower to mow the neighbor's lawn and in return, he would pay them 20% of the profit for borrowing their lawn mower. He started mowing about five lawns a week and making some good money for a high school kid. As word of mouth spread, he started to get more and more requests for his lawn mowing service and realized he did not have the manpower to keep up with all the requests. At this point he had about $500 saved up and decided to buy two more lawn mowers. He asked a couple of his friends if they wanted to join his business but they would have to pay him 20% of their profit for using his lawn mower. Eventually this kid had saved a ton of money and started a somewhat successful business in our neighborhood. He eventually went to college for business and stopped his lawn mowing business but I assume he has probably made it as a successful entrepreneur, due to his work ethic and motivation to succeed.

When most people think about opening a business this is where their mind goes. If you love your current job and think you can do it better than the business you are working for then that may be a great avenue for a business. You then can cut out the middleman and become the owner. Let's say you are a really good construction worker and you have enough knowledge and experience to get your contractor's license. You can open up a construction business and now instead of getting paid hourly you can go and give the bids and keep the whole paycheck minus taxes and insurance of course.

When opening a local business, you will want to follow the outline above and before opening the new business make sure there is an actual need for your services. That way you know it will be successful before you even start. You may want to chat with family and friends and see what they think, pay for a local Google ad and see if people are interested, and look around your area and see what the competition will be. Once you know if your business will be successful then you can move on to the next steps.

- Will you need to rent a space or can you run the business out of your home?

- What will you need to buy to start this business?

- Do you need any employees starting out or can you

run it yourself at the start?

• How much money will you need to start up?

Make sure you are following local guidelines and do a lot of research before starting a business.

Become A Content Creator: Podcasting, Youtube, Blogger, Influencer, Etc.

Tim Ferriss, a widely known podcaster, influenced me greatly and got me into the success mindset. Tim Ferriss today has a very successful podcast, YouTube channel, and has written extremely successful books such as the *Four-Hour Work Week* and *Tools of Titans*.

Tim Ferriss is one of my favorite examples of a content creator. He built his business solely off of the content he created. He took the knowledge in his brain and transferred it to different platforms to teach people what he very well understands. He is now a widely known very successful public figure and he got his start by essentially being a content creator. I like to use Tim as an example because typically when we think of content creators we think of "influencers."

A content creator can create content on how to properly put on make-up or someone like Tim who is sharing tips for success. Neither option is right or wrong and it all depends on your knowledge and what you can bring to the platforms that are out there. Anyone can create some income with the phone in their pocket right now. Yes, having constant access to technology has its cons but it has opened up so many new opportunities, especially for a young entrepreneur. Creating content takes $0 and some people are able to be really successful with it. If you are able to create content people want to consume, then you may have an opportunity on your hands. There are many different kinds of content creators: life coaches, influencers, bloggers, podcasters, youtubers, etc. Any platform where you can create content and have followers or subscribers will fit into this category.

How to become a content creator:

1. Pick your content topic

What will your content be about? Try and find a niche so you can target a certain demographic of people. Pick a topic that you are very knowledgeable about and have experience in.

2. Identify your "Fane Base"

Think about who will be "following" you. This can be social media followers or subscribers to your blog, podcast, or YouTube channel. Your fan base should be based on who will be interested in the content you are creating. You will be able to use this knowledge to attract those people to your content so they can become followers or subscribers.

3. Find a way to make money off your content

Now that you have a good idea of what type of content you want to create you need to find a way to capitalize on it. For instance, if you are using Instagram as your primary tool and you get 20,000 followers but have no way to capitalize then you may be "Insta Famous" but let's face it, you're still broke.

Monetization: Most of the time to make money off of monetization (money you get for a view or click of a video or post) you need to have a lot of followers. If you do not have a large audience then this will take a long time to make some money off of but hopefully eventually you will be able to capitalize on monetization.

Subscription: Sites like Instagram, YouTube, and different podcast platforms have a paid subscription service where you get a percentage of the money each month for your paid subscribers. If you create your own website or blog and have paid content subscription, you can cut the middle man out and keep the whole percentage yourself. Create valuable content that will engage more people to subscribe to your service. As you keep creating, your number of subscribers will grow as well as your income.

Sponsors: Once you get a large enough audience, you can find different sponsors that pay you for advertising their products. This can be utilized in pretty much any content you create. Some sponsors may offer you a percentage of anyone who uses your link to buy a product or some sponsors may pay you per post or mention.

Selling: The last way to make money off of your content is to sell something. You can sell anything you make or create. Maybe you created a short very informative video and offer it to your followers for a small price. The other way to make money off of selling is to sell a product someone else made and take a percentage. Similar to some sponsorship programs, you can sell items for a business and can keep a percentage of each sell.

4. Promote yourself

Free Promotion Ideas: Let all your friends and family know that you are doing this new thing and ask them to share and support your content. Consistently posting content will increase your chances of being seen by more people. You may also find forums, similar sites, or pages and interreact with people on those sites to attract them to your content. As you keep spreading the word and being consistent in your content, your subscribers and followers will grow.

Paid promotion ideas: You can pay for Google ads or Facebook ads. These are a great way to get interested parties to your content. With these ads you are able to target the people who would be most interested in your content and have a higher chance of growing your subscribers and followers.

Technology has advanced so much throughout the years and has opened up a door for entrepreneurs to create online material. You can become a life coach, host a podcast, create a YouTube channel, write a blog, or even become an influencer. If you are very knowledgeable about something and want to share it with the world, take advantage of the online platforms that technology has made available and capitalize on them.

High-Cost Cash-Flowing Business Ideas:

These cash-flowing business ideas typically take some capital to get started. If you have the lending and or the capital to start one of these, it may be a good option. Even if you currently do not have the means to start one of these, I still encourage you to read through them to see if you may be interested in one of these ideas in the future.

Laundromat or Carwash

Both a laundromat and carwash can create pretty passive income if done right. You can make both automated if you put suitable systems in place. You will have to hire someone to clean or collect the cash earnings each week, but it might be worth looking into if you have the capital to start one of these businesses.

Storage Units

Storage units are something I have always wanted to get into. They remind me a lot of real estate in the sense that people rent space from you, but you do not have the same laws and hoops you have to jump through. You can pretty much automate a storage unit with the right systems in place and collect money each month from the people who need storage.

Vending Machines

Vending machines are completely passive from the start. The hardest thing about vending machines is finding a place to put them. Most companies will have their own vending machines or charge a hefty fee. You will have to stock the vending machines and collect the money, but vending machines can be very passive. It is definitely worth looking into if you have a place to put vending machines or know somewhere that might cut you a deal.

Business chains

Business chains are fantastic because they come with a blueprint for what to do. Large chains have tested different methods and will hand you a blueprint of how to succeed with that business. You will want to look into the chain itself, see what fees are associated with it, and consider if that chain will be successful in the area you are planning. Business chains come in all sorts, and you can find something that fits your passion. Starting a business chain takes a lot of capital but can be very lucrative.

There are so many different business ideas you can make money off of. If you find something you're good at or passionate about, turn it into an income stream and then figure out how to turn that income passive. Creating passive income is one of the secrets to early retirement, and if you can figure out a way to do that by talking about or sharing something you are passionate about, it will be much better than working for someone else your entire life.

Your Turn To Think Of A Business Idea:

1. What are two topics you are knowledgeable about and or interested in?

a.

b.

c.

2. What is a problem or need each one of these topics presents? Try and think outside the box and find a need for each topic.

a.

b.

c.

3. What business category does each topic fit into? Online service, creating a product, creating content, etc.

a.

b.

c.

4. How will you make money off of each topic?

a.

b.

c.

CHAPTER 14: DIVE INTO REAL ESTATE

Lucy: What is it that you want?

Charlie Brown: Real estate!

—*from Charles Schulz's A Charlie Brown Christmas (1965)*

Picture this. Two identical 25-year olds have the same job and $15,000 saved in the bank. Person A uses the $15,000 for a down payment on a house with a monthly payment of $2,000 a month. Person B decides to put the money in a savings account and continue renting at $2,000 a month. Thirty years later, Person A has a house that is paid off and Person B has some money in a savings account and their rent has increased to $4,000 a month for rent. If the proper steps are followed, Person A is going to be way better off because they bought a house they could afford. If Person B put their savings into investments, it may be a different story but instead, Person B is paying more in rent 30 years later and most likely can't retire with the money person B has saved up. Person A is close to retirement and Person B will probably be working a lot longer or living on government support. This is a hypothetical story but there is validity to it. If as a young adult you take the property introductory steps into real estate you will most likely be a lot better off down the line financially.

Real estate is my bread and butter and one of the main reasons I have been able to build wealth so fast. I will be writing a whole book on real estate one day, but for now, here is one chapter on one of the greatest things America has to offer.

Real estate is so amazing because truly anyone can build wealth with real estate. Wealthy people as well as young, savvy investors can use real estate as a wealth building engine. A young investor will typically start with less savings and will have to put in more time and work to be successful in real estate, whereas a wealthy person who has a lot of capital can invest in real estate with little to zero effort because they can hire other people to do the heavy lifting. In my opinion, real estate, if done correctly, is less risky than other investment strategies. When investing in real estate if you stay within your means and buy places where the numbers pencil out, you should make money. There are simple rules and procedures you will need to follow to minimize the risk, but if you educate yourself and buy good properties, you will love real estate.

Four Ways To Make Money In Real Estate

1. Cash Flow

In real estate, cash flow is simply your net income after all expenses are paid. If you calculate this number correctly, you essentially would be able to go and spend all of your "cashflow" money and your real estate would not be affected. My goal was to have enough cashflow coming in every month that I didn't have to work. After a few years of hard work, I was able to make that happen. Cash flow is one of the most important numbers when analyzing a deal because it will be the monthly income of your property.

If you buy a property that has a negative cash flow and you cannot supplement the difference each month, you will soon be in a very difficult position. On the other hand, if you buy a property that has a positive cash flow and pays for itself each month, you will not have to stress about making a payment each month on the property and eventually; you will get a property for free (because your tenant makes your payments).

How to analyze cash flow in deals?

To find out how much a property cashflows do the following steps.

1. Find the gross income.

2. Subtract the mortgage, taxes, insurance, 10% for property management, 10% for capital expenditures, and any other expenses.

3. The remaining amount is your cashflow.

Always make sure to buy properties that have a positive cash flow, especially if you are a new investor. It is really easy to find yourself upside-down in an investment if you do not do your due diligence correctly.

2. Appreciation

Appreciation is the value of the property growing over time. On average, homes will appreciate 3% every year over a 10-year period. So, if you buy a house and hold it for 10 years, you can assume it will be worth 30% more at the end of that 10 years. Appreciation occurs for different reasons and can change from market to market. The value of a house is typically related to the demand of the market where the house is located. This is the reason that houses are so expensive in cities where a lot of people want to live.

Appreciation can also be increased due to inflation because as things cost higher, houses become more expensive to build, and in turn that will increase the demand for previously built houses. In addition, each generation of humans in America is bigger than the last which means we need more houses to hold everyone. As more and more humans look for housing, the demand for housing increases.

3. Principal Reduction

One of the greatest things about real estate is even if you find a property that just breaks even or maybe even loses some money each month, in the long run you are still making money. Each month your tenants are paying down the principal on your property loan. Even if you have to supplement some of the costs each month with your own money, each time a tenant pays rent, the tenant is paying towards your property. For example, if you buy a 4-plex for $500,000 on a 30-year loan and you break even every month on your expenses. You may not have any monthly cash flow but in 30 years your tenants have paid off your $500,000 loan plus you have most likely accumulated at least another $450,000 in appreciation. So even though in this example you did not make any money for 30 years, at the end of 30 years you have at least $950,000 in equity on your property and it was paid for by your tenants.

4. Tax Benefits

One of the greatest benefits of real estate is the tax benefits you receive. Real estate provides so many different tax benefits and makes it one of the best investments you can buy.

Tax Deduction on Mortgage Interest: As a real estate investor, you can deduct all of the interest on the mortgage you pay each year on your investment property from your taxable income.

Property Tax Deduction: You can deduct property taxes for your property from your taxable income.

Capital Gains Exclusion: If the property you buy is a primary residence, you can exclude up to $250,000 in capital gains from your taxable income and if you are married you can exclude $500,000.

Depreciation Deduction: You can depreciate your rental property over a period of 27.5 years, which will reduce your taxable income.

Investment Expenses: You can deduct almost all expenses related to managing your investment property, such as repairs, insurance, and travel.

1031 Exchange: If you want to use the capital in one of your properties to buy a new one you can defer your capital gains taxes by using a 1031 exchange.

The tax benefits of real estate investment make real estate a great investment choice. Make sure to chat with a CPA and understand the different tax benefits when investing in real estate.

Find Deals With All Four Benefits

You want to try and find deals with cash flow, appreciation, principal reduction, and tax benefits. For example, let's say someone buys a house for $250,000, and the house cash flows $200 a month from renting it out each month. After 10 years, the owner has not had to pay a payment on the property and has made $24,000 over the years in cash flow. On top of that, the property is now worth $325,000. Even though $200 cash flow does not seem like a lot, it adds up over time, and after 10 years, in this example, the home buyer made $99,000 due to principal reduction and cashflow.

Now imagine that the property bought in the last example cash flows $1,500 a month at the end of 10 years the buyer made $255,000 in profit plus all the tax benefits that come along with owning real estate. You can write off a loss on your taxes of up to $25,000 each year in expenses and depreciation (as of 2022). So essentially, that $25,000 write-off can counteract directly with your other income from a business or a W2 job. There are many other tax benefits in real estate, but it differs for everyone. If you buy a property that has cash flow, appreciation, principal reduction, and tax benefits, you will do well in real estate.

Five Types Of Investment Properties

When talking about real estate, there are different types of investments, and it is essential to differentiate between them and understand the level of risk involved in each one. How much time you have to work on a property or your end goals will determine what type of real estate you should get into.

1. Long Term Rentals

Long term rentals are a great source of income. Essentially you could rent out any type of investment property. You could rent out a place you bought that was turn-key (no work needed), you could rent out a home you had to fix up before renting, or you could rent out a fix and flip if you cannot sell it right away.

Long Term Rentals give you a buffer to make your payments. If you have a positive cash flow, you can potentially hold that property as long as you want/need before selling it because the tenants are paying your bills.

3 types of long-term rentals:

Single-family housing:

Single-family housing can be amazing if you find the right long term renters for that house. If you are able to find good tenants you can potentially see a lot of income in this type of rental. The downside to a single-family home is that you only have one tenant. If that tenant doesn't pay or moves out, the bills fall directly back on you. If you get into single-family housing, make sure you set aside enough money each month to prepare for a vacancy.

Multi-unit 2-4:

Multi-units are great because you can still get a conventional loan and put little money down, but you have more tenants. Unlike single-family housing, if you have a vacancy with multi-family, the other units rented out may cover the costs. The downside can be that you have to deal with more people, and more units, and the turnover rate might be higher than a single-family home.

Apartments 5-MAX:

Apartments are the way to go if you are in the money-making business. You will have to get a commercial loan which is a little more complicated, but can be worth it. If you buy an apartment, you will want to hire someone to manage it full-time unless you feel you are qualified. You should have enough people renting that you are always making money. However, keep in mind there are more units, and more things will need to be fixed so put aside money in your capital expenditures.

2. Short Term Rentals

Short-term rentals are becoming more and more popular. You can do a short-term rental with any house or unit you own as long as there are no regulations forbidding short-term rentals in your city. Sites like Airbnb and VRBO have made short-term rentals a reality in most markets, and it seems as if they are here to stay. I have a short-term rental and it has a great return, but it does take more work. Short-term rentals will typically have a higher net income but as the owner, there is a lot more you have to do versus a typical long-term investment. You have to furnish the house and make it look nice, coordinate the cleaners and the handyman, as well as book and manage all of the renters. Most of the time being a short-term manager is pretty straightforward but sometimes people do throw parties, break stuff, or are super high maintenance. If you chose this option, it is important to either hire someone to manage or make sure you have plenty of time and resources to do a good job at it.

3. Fix and Flips

Fix and flips are where someone buys a beat-up house for cheap, fixes it up, and then sells it for more than what they bought it for. The buyer must stay under budget to make this option worth it, and if the buyer goes over budget, they will lose money. Fix and flips are a little riskier because if the market drops, the buyer may not be able to sell the property for profit. This can be a good option if you are able to get the work done cheap. If you have experience and the time to fix up a house it would be a lot easier to stay under budget versus hiring someone else to do all of it. When choosing this option, make sure to work with a real estate agent to help you determine the value of the house before and after renovations.

4. Fix and Hold

Fix and holds are if fix and flips and rentals had a baby. The buyer fixes up the property and then rents out the property for income. Then when the time is right the buyer may choose to sell this property down the line for a profit. Fix and holds are a little less risky than just fix and flips because the buyer has a backup plan if something goes south. The buyer can rent it out, and wait until selling will be profitable.

Reasons to hold a property:

· Hold for one year to avoid a heavy tax hit.

· Hold until you made some money back in cashflow.

· Hold your primary residence for two years to possibly avoid all taxes associated with that property.

· Hold until the property appreciates.

5. Buy and Hold

Buy and hold is essentially buying a property in good condition and holding onto it. This can be your primary residence (the home you live in) or a rental. It is always a good long-term investment if you can find a good deal on a house that will appreciate over time.

Tax tip: If you live in the house for at least two years within the last five years as your primary residence, you do not have to pay capital gains on up to $250,000 in profit for a single person and $500,000 in profit for a married couple. After you have lived in it for two years, you can then rent it out and buy another home to live in and watch the appreciation grow on both of your houses. You can repeat this process as often as you want, and then when you want to sell, you will save a TON of money on taxes.

Three Tips To Finding Good Deals

Being able to find good deals will make or break a real estate investor. If you do not find and buy good deals you will probably fail, or at the least not be as successful. It is important to educate yourself and get into deals that will make you money in the long run.

1. Location

Location is a key aspect in finding a good deal, and it depends on what you are looking for. Things such as crime rate, schools, population, and job opportunity are all things you will want to consider when thinking about investing in an area. The location you pick will determine the type of tenants you get, which can make all the difference in real estate.

2. Connections

It is vital to make connections. If you can make good connections with key players in real estate, you will have a better chance at finding good on and off-market deals.

Real estate agent:

Find a local real estate agent you can work with. Real estate agents will know the area well and help you get into a location that fits your needs. Real estate agents can set you up with an automatic email for any properties that come on the market that fit what you are looking for.

Keep in mind that you do not have to use a real estate agent and there are other options out there but if you can find a good agent, they will add a lot of value to your business.

Contractors:

Contractors often work with people who are in real estate. When someone wants to sell their house, they will usually have a contractor come in to fix the place up. If you get in good with a contractor and let them know what you are looking for, they may find you an excellent off-market deal without even needing a real estate agent.

Property managers:

Property managers can help you with your rentals, and they usually help a lot of other owners too. Let the property management company know that you are looking at buying another place, and they might be able to set you up to buy a home from one of their clients who want to sell.

Loan Officer:

Find good loan officers you can trust and rely on for your personal real estate deals, but they also work with many others who want to buy and sell houses. Let them know that you are looking, and they could bring you an excellent off-market deal.

3. Use Free Resources

There are many free resources out there for people who want to get into real estate. There are resources for learning and understanding but also for finding great deals.

BiggerPockets: I love to use BiggerPockets to grow my knowledge. You can download the app or go to their website. Participate in the forums, listen to their podcast, and watch different videos BiggerPockets provides.

Zillow/Realtor/Redfin: If you do not have an agent in the area, these websites are a great way to see what houses are for sale. You can also see the houses that are for sale by the owner (meaning they do not have a real estate agent). If you are interested in investing in an area, these websites would be a great start.

Loopnet: LoopNet is an excellent resource if you are interested in commercial real estate, business, or properties over 5 units. Loopnet is similar to Zillow/Realtor/Redfin but for commercial properties.

Others: There are many free resources out there, including podcasts, videos, and books on the topic of real estate. Take advantage of them.

Loan Options In Real Estate

There are many types of loans out there to take advantage of, and I will outline the most popular ones and how you can use them to your advantage.

Conventional:

A conventional loan is my go-to when investing in anything under four units. You can use a conventional loan for a single-family home and complex up to four units. You do not get as good of interest rates as an FHA loan, but there are fewer hoops you have to jump through and the mortgage insurance will be less expensive when using a conventional loan. For a primary residence (when you will live at the home), you usually will have to put down 5% of the total price. For an investment property (where you are not going to live there), you typically have to put down 15-25% depending on the lender. Conventional loans have different term options ranging from 5 to 30 years; most people usually do 30 years.

FHA

An FHA loan is used for a single-family home to anything up to a 4-plex. With an FHA loan, the property must meet specific standards, and a special inspection needs to be done. When using an FHA loan, make sure the property fits the criteria and if not, look into a conventional loan. Using an FHA loan for a primary residence, you usually only have to put down 3-5% of the total purchase price. FHA loans have different term options ranging from 5-30 years; most people typically do 30-year loans.

VA Loans

If you were in the military, they offer great loan options, and some are so awesome that you can get away with putting 0% down. Meaning you can essentially buy a house for $0. If you were in the military, make sure to look into VA loans. Interest rates with a VA loan are typically .5%-1% better than conventional loans and you do not have to pay mortgage insurance. If you have access to a VA loan it is an incredible product and should be your first choice.

Commercial

Commercial loans are needed to purchase any business or complex with 5 or more units. Commercial loans usually have 5-20 year term options, and every 5 years, the rate will change. Every commercial loan is different, and honestly, in my experience, the most complex loan to get when you are starting out. However, once you find an excellent commercial lender to work with, getting commercial loans becomes a lot easier.

DSCR Loans

DSCR loans are new to me but amazing. I did my first DCSR loan this year and I really love it. You can use a DSCR loan for almost any investment property if you find a lender who will do it. The rate is typically about 1-1.5 points higher than a conventional loan, but instead of going off your debt-to-income ratio they go off of the income potential of the property. The other cool thing about a DSCR loan if that you can place the property directly under an LLC.

Hard money loans

Hard money loans are fantastic but come with risks. Hard money lenders will let you put little to nothing down but give you super-high interest rates. If you want to use hard money or private money lenders, make sure you do your research and find out if it is right for you. Hard money lenders are typically used when someone doesn't have the cash to buy a property. Then after the person fixes the property up or brings value to it, they will refinance it under a conventional loan and get better interest rates. This strategy is known as the BRRR strategy, and if you want to learn more about it, research the BRRR strategy.

Seller financing

Seller financing is when the seller is the lender. Typically for this to work, the seller has to own the house outright, and you pay them as the bank. When doing this, you will need a lawyer to write up a note, and the property should be under your name if done correctly. Seller finance is great because you and the seller can determine how you want the loan set up. You can get better rates and if you cannot qualify for a loan for some reason, seller financing is always an option.

How To Analyze A Property

It is crucial to get good at analyzing deals. The more deals you study, whether you buy them or not, the better you will understand how to analyze a deal.

1. About the property

First, you will want to look at the property itself.

- What year was it built?

- How many bedrooms and baths and is there an opportunity to add more?

- What is the price? Could you possibly get the property for less?

- Can you add value to the property? If so, what would the estimated price of the property be after the improvements?

2. Loan

Next, you will look at the loan you will need to buy it.

If you have a lender you work with, they will answer these questions for you. If you do not have a lender, free websites will give you estimated numbers.

- What type of loan can you get?
- What will the mortgage be?
- What will the Interest rate be?
- How much are Insurance and taxes if not included in your mortgage?

3. Income

Next, you will want to look at the income on the property. This will mainly apply if you are planning on renting out the property. If you are hoping for appreciation, it is still a good idea to look at the rental income. If you are unsure how much the property would rent, look at rentometer as a guide for how much you can rent each unit out.

- What will the predicted rent be?
- Is there any other income (washers/dryers, garage space, etc.)?

4. Expenses

Expenses happen whether you want them or not, and you need to plan for that when analyzing deals.

- Will you use a property management company? That will usually be 6-10% of your gross rental income.
- Will you have a maintenance guy, yard maintenance, snow How much will utilities be each month?

• Prepare for expenses, you will want to set aside 10% of your gross income for vacancy, repairs, and capital expenditures (big expenses you will have down the line).

5. Major repairs

You want to account for any major repairs, you will need to fix after buying the property.

• Are there major repairs required?

• If so, what is required, and approximately how much will it cost?

6. Find your final numbers

Cash flow:

Subtract your total expenses, mortgage, taxes, and insurance from your total monthly income to find your cash flow (major repairs will be calculated in the Cash on Cash ROI). Positive cash flow is ideal, but if you think the property will cash flow after 1 or 2 years and have the cash reserves, it may still be a good option.

Cap rate:

To find your cap rate, you will take the total net income for the year (not including your mortgage costs) and divide that by the sales price. Properties 6-12% are generally good cap rates, and anything higher is going to be a great cap rate.

Cash on Cash Return on Investment:

For the cash-on-cash ROI, you will take your NET

yearly income and divide that by the total of your down payment and major repair costs. 12-20% ROI is generally really good. Anything higher is great.

Improvement value:

Lastly, if you are making improvements or your goal is to fix and flip, you should look at the property's value after you are done. What is the estimated new value of the property after renovations? What is your net income after selling? Take your gross income (equity gained in sale and any other rental income earned while owned) and subtract it from your total expenses (expenses, mortgage, insurance, taxes, major repairs, realtor fees, and any other costs).

How To Make Money Off Living In A House

If you want to get into real estate, your personal living situation is a great place to start. If you are currently renting why not buy a home to live in and get some roommates or renters to help with your mortgage? You must be smart about buying a house and know what you are getting into, but buying is a lot better than renting in the long run.

Buy a home as your primary residence

When you buy a house as your primary residence you only have to put down 3-5% of the cost of the property. You can buy anything up to a 4-plex as your primary residence.

Make money off a single-family home

If you want to get into a single-family home, roommates

would be the way to make money. You can buy the house with 3-5% down, and as long as your roommates pay more than your mortgage, you have a great deal. Let's say you bought a four bed two bath house for $300,000, and your mortgage was $1,750 a month. You find three roommates that pay $750 each, and you all split the utilities. You will be making $500 each month, you will be living for free, and your roommates are paying off your home.

Make money off a multi-family home

If you want to get into a multi-unit up to a 4-plex, you can rent out the units you are not in. Let's say you buy a 4-plex for $375,000, and your mortgage is $2,000 a month. You rent out three units for $1,000 each, and they pay their own utilities. Now you are making $1,000 a month, plus living for free, and your tenants are paying off your house. Now, let's say you get a roommate for $500 a month; that is even more money in your pocket each month.

Make money off a fixer upper

You can also find a home that is a fixer-upper. Sometimes it is tough to find properties that have cash flow in some cities. If that is the case in your area, a fixer-upper may be the way to go. After you fix the property up, you can live in it, sell it, have roommates, or rent it out.

Repeat

With any of these options after you have lived in the property for at least a year, you can essentially go and buy another house with 3-5% down to move into and fully rent out your previous house. You can repeat this process over and over again if you please and this is one of the best ways to build up your portfolio.

Four things to keep in mind when starting in real estate

1. When starting, never buy something you cannot pay the mortgage on each month with your regular job.

2. Get creative when looking at properties to see how you can make money from them.

3. Try to find places with cash flow, and if not, buy fixer-uppers that will cash flow once fixed.

4. Research the type of loan you are getting and understand your options.

Just do it

If real estate is something you want to get into, you just have to just do it. I was terrified of buying my first house, but now I am grateful I bought when I did. Start to do more research and start looking at properties, even if it is just on Zillow or realtor.com. Find out if you would be more interested in flips, holds, or rentals. Try and start taking little steps to becoming a real estate investor.

4 Small steps you can take to get started in real estate

1. Start analyzing deals

2. Start listening to podcasts and reading articles

3. Start talking with real estate agents and looking at different properties

4. Start looking at a house to buy to live in and create cash flow

How can you get started in real estate?

1. What option works best for you right now?

a. Buy a primary residence and rent out extra rooms and units

b. Buy an investment property with 25% down

c. Neither. I need to first save up some money and chat with a lender

2. What is 1 small action you can take to start toward this step?

Ex: Get pre-qualified with a lender, chat with a realtor, go look at properties, etc.

3. Make a game plan. Write 5 steps you can take to complete the option you chose.

1.

2.

3.

4.

5.

CHAPTER 15: BUILD WEALTH WITH INVESTING

Compound interest is the eighth wonder of the world. He who understands it, earns it. He who doesn't, pays it.

— *Albert Einstein*

I nvesting in stocks, retirement funds, or any IRAs can be very overwhelming and scary. In my first three months as a teacher, I had to decide what retirement path I wanted to go down and once I chose I could not change my path. I had three options. Option 1 was to have only a 401k. Option 2 was to be in the pension fund and the 401k. Option 3 was to only be in the pension. As a young adult, brand new teacher, and brand new to investing, this was a very overwhelming decision and I went with the second option.

If I could do it all over again, I would have done the 401k option because I only taught for four years and the pension fund is not going to do me much good. I wish I had the options laid out more clearly for me and had more time to make that decision.

I have learned more over the past five years and started investing not only for retirement but also for passive income. I max out my Roth IRA every year by putting $6,000 into my account. I also invest monthly into an eREIT called Fundrise, a Robo advisor, and some stocks I believe will stay around for a while like Apple, Amazon, Home Depot, and Visa. I am not dependent on any of my investments, but I look at all of my investments as a backup plan for retirement and an extra income source. I try and reinvest all of the money I make off of investments for now to grow my investment portfolio as much as possible.

This chapter is meant to give you a basic understanding of the different investments that are available. Being diverse in your overall investments is a tried-and-true practice among the wealthy. Investing in the stock market, a Roth IRA, or a 401K is a long process, and it can take a very long time to get a good yield on your investments.

When most people think about investing, they tend to believe that they are investing for retirement. You should invest for retirement but also try and invest for some extra passive income. Setting up your investments, you should have money allocated to retirement (long-term) investments each month and then have money allocated to creating passive income each month.

Five types of investments

1. Stock

Stocks are essentially a fraction of ownership in a company. Once a company goes public, anyone can buy or trade stocks for that company. If you purchase shares in a company and five years later, that company is 10x in value, and your stock will be 10x in value, and you could yield a significant profit. On the other hand, if you buy stocks in a company and the value of that company drops, you will lose money and not be able to sell your shares for what you bought them for.

A cool benefit of investing in the stock market is choosing what company you want to buy shares in and how many shares. If you feel you have a good idea of what companies will be very successful, this could be great. On the other hand, it is very easy to lose a lot of money in the stock market. There is risk involved, so make sure you calculate the risk when investing in individual stocks.

There are a couple of ways you can invest in stocks. You can use free apps such as Robinhood, JP Morgan, and E*trade to invest in individual stocks or invest in a Robo-advisor. A Robo-advisor will assess your risks, goals, and the amount of money you want to put in and then buy shares for you that fit your needs. The average return of a Robo-advisor is 2.5% per year.

The other option is to use a stockbroker. Stockbrokers will typically only want to work with you if you have a large amount of capital to put into stocks. When choosing a stockbroker to work with, make sure they are qualified and I always try and go off of referrals. The average return of a stockbroker is 10% per year (Royal 2022).

2. eREITs

An eREIT is a real estate investment trust or fund that makes money specifically in real estate. You can buy into an eREIT and get a yield on how well that specific fund is making money each year. eREITSs are a representation of the real estate market. If the real estate market is continually going up, the eREIT will also increase. Real estate has been fairly stable over the last 100 years and has increased over time. There have been dips in the real estate market here and there, but it always bounces back within a few years.

A disadvantage of an eREIT is that if the company makes poor decisions, you can be out of all of the money you invested quickly. However, if you invest in a company with different long-term and short-term options, as long as you can leave your money in the eREIT, you should eventually yield a reasonable return.

I view most eREITs as less risky than other stocks because real estate has proven to increase in price over time. However, it also depends on the company you invest in so make sure you do your research.

There are different eREIT companies, and the one I use is Fundrise. Fundrise allows you to start investing with as little as $100 down, and Fundrise has an average annual yield of 9-11%.

You can get bonus shares on Fundrise if you use this link to sign up: www.joceyj.com/fundrise

3. 401Ks

A 401K is offered by many employers and is a retirement savings plan. If your employer offers a 401K, it is worth looking into because there are some tax advantages. You agree what percent of your paycheck will go directly into your 401K, and the money will go into your 401K savings account before it is taxed.

Some employers offer great benefits like matching the amount you put into your 401K each month. This is a great benefit but look into the vesting period if you plan not to work at that job for a long time. Many employers will have a vesting period where you only get the money the employer contributed if you work for the company for a certain number of years. There are also self-directed 401ks available and if you are self-employed, this may be a good option for you to look into to save for retirement.

Keep in mind that it is a long-term savings account when you put money into your 401k. You will not be able to access this money for a long time, and if you do, there may be penalties.

4. IRA account

An IRA account is an individual retirement savings account. You can open an IRA account through a bank, broker, investment company, and even some employers offer IRAs in their retirement plan. There are different types of IRAs: Traditional, Roth, Simple, and SEP. They all have their distinctions from each other, and if you want to invest in an IRA, I suggest you look into each one. IRAs offer significant tax benefits, but you cannot take money out until 59.5 years of age. If withdrawn before 59.5

years of age, you will be hit with a 10% tax penalty.

There are income limitations to who can invest in IRAs and how much you can invest, but when starting on your journey to success, it is good to put some money into an IRA each year to prepare for retirement one day.

5. Cryptocurrency

Cryptocurrency is becoming more and more popular. Crypto can be very confusing and misunderstood. Basically, cryptocurrency is a digital currency that is secured by cryptography. Cryptocurrency was made to be a suitable replacement for money because you cannot print more of it (unlike money), and there is a finite amount (unlike money). Crypto works like stocks as it can gain or lose value, but crypto can also be treated like money to pay for things or send someone money.

There are different types of coins. The first and most notable is Bitcoin. Some believe that everyone will pay for things with bitcoin or other coins one day, and some believe that eventually, it will disappear. There is no absolute on either side, but some people are getting very wealthy as early investors in cryptocurrency.

If you want to invest in crypto, you MUST research and learn about it. You will have to spend hours to grasp what cryptocurrency is, and you still will have a lot of questions. It is a good idea to diversify your portfolio, and crypto is an area you should look more into.

Small Steps To Investing:

Set up a Roth IRA:

Set up a Roth IRA either with your employer or a self-directed Roth IRA. Try and contribute at least $100 a month, if possible, contribute $500 a month to invest $6,000 (the maximum limit) each year. You will be able to access your money when you are 59-1/2 and using a Roth IRA is a great way to save for retirement.

Contribute to your 401k:

If your employer offers a 401k this can be a great option for saving for retirement. Even if you only put $50 in your 401k each month, it will make a difference in the long run.

Open a brokerage account:

You can open a brokerage account and invest in stocks, funds, eREITS, etc. When investing in any stocks make sure to do your due diligence and be prepared to hold that stock as long as possible. Be smart and do not tie up more money than you should into stocks. Make sure you have a good amount of cash savings always put aside.

Start Small:

As you are learning to invest in any of these options, start small. Get your feet wet with a small amount of money and then once you understand more about what type of investor you are, you can start putting more money into those investments.

Seek Advice:

As with anything in life, it is important to seek advice from experts. You can read articles or do your own research on the internet. Most brokerages offer a free consolation and that could give you a good idea of where to start as well.

Get Started In Investing

Pick 3 types of Investments to learn more about:

1.

2.

3.

Research each type of investment and pick two that you want to open:

1.

2.

Do you want to contribute to the account on a monthly basis or yearly basis?

1.

2.

How much do you want to contribute each month or year?

1.

2.

YOUR TURN TO FIND SUCCESS!

CHAPTER 16: YOUR TURN

The only thing standing between you and your goal is the bullshit story you keep telling yourself as to why you can't achieve it.

—Jordan Belfort from the 2013 film, The Wolf of the Wall Street

First, let's review the five pillars to find success and financial freedom:

Principle 1: Find your WHY. You have to know your WHY. Otherwise, you will not have any motivation to succeed.

Principle 2: Live healthy. You must have good mental, physical, and social health on your journey to financial freedom.

Principle 3: Gain Knowledge. You must have knowledge about your work, business interest, and skills to be successful. You also should try and always obtain new information that will help you on your journey.

Principle 4: Money Management. You must be able to make money, save money, budget money, and build a good credit score to become financially free.

Principle 5: Create Passive Income. You must create passive income through entrepreneurship, real estate, or investments. Then you will truly have financial freedom.

Once you start on your journey and start to have some financial success make sure to still focus on your health, knowledge, and money management. Once you find some financial success, it is easy to lose yourself in that success and forget to focus on the fundamentals you learned in this book.

To avoid having to reset or take a backward step on your journey, make sure to remember the importance of your health, knowledge, and money management.

Now you get to create a five-year plan! You can use the worksheet in this book or the worksheet in the free online workbook for this book (you can download it at www.joceyj.com/breakfreereader). This five-year plan is a great start to your journey and each year make sure to sit down and update your five-year plan each year.

Create A Five-Year Plan

1. Identify what step are you at now.

2. Is there anything you want to be better at? Example: social health, reading, making money, money management, etc.

3. Where do you want to be in 5 years? Example: I want to create $1,000 monthly passive income in 5 years, I want to be able to retire in 5 years, or I want to have my master's degree in 5 years.

4. Now create a five-year plan outline to help guide you in your journey.

You will list where you want to be in each category for that year.

Health will include social, mental, and physical health. Health is where you can put fitness/nutrition goals, family goals, friend goals, etc.

Knowledge is where you will put degree goals, reading goals, learning goals, etc.

Money/work is where you will put what you want to be doing for work, how much money you want to save, different money strategies, etc.

Money-making creations is where you will put things you have created, how much passive income they are bringing in, or even things you might want to start on even if they are not bringing in money.

Year 1 (The end of this year):

Health:

Knowledge:

Money/Work:

Money making creation:

Year 2:

Health:

Knowledge:

Money/Work:

Money making creation:

Year 3:

Health:

Knowledge:

Money/Work:

Money making creation:

Year 4:

Health:

Knowledge:

Money/Work:

Money making creation:

Year 5:

Health:

Knowledge:

Money/Work:

Money making creation:

THANK YOU!

Dear Reader,

Congratulations on creating a five-year plan, and congratulations on finishing this book. Only 20% of people will finish a book to the end, so that is a considerable accomplishment on your part. You want success, and you want to learn, and that is what it takes to find financial freedom in this world. It is going to be hard, and it will bring a lot of challenges, but I know you can do it.

Find your WHY, know what is driving you to success, and stick to it. Never stop learning and growing as you are on this journey. Anything is possible in this world if you are willing to work hard for it. Take the initiative for your life and set yourself up for success starting now.

If you take anything away from this book, remember this:

Someday is not a day of the week. *Someday* is now. Now go get started!

Thank you for joining me on this journey to finding financial freedom, and I hope you have learned some valuable life lessons. I would love to hear what you have to say, you can reach me by email at breakfreereader@joceyj.com

Also, I would greatly appreciate it if you would take the time and leave a review on Amazon about the book.

Thank you for reading

Jocelyn Kaufman

REFERENCES

"Alcohol and Substance Misuse." 2020. Centers for Disease Control and Prevention, Centers for Disease Control and Prevention. Last modified 03 Nov 2020. https://www.cdc.gov/workplacehealthpromotion/tools-resources/workplace-health/alcohol-substance-misuse.html.

Coulson, J.C., Jim McKenna, and M. Field. (2008). Exercising at work and self-reported work performance. *International Journal of Workplace Health Management*, no. 1: 176-197. https://doi.org/10.1108/17538350810926534.

Gillis. Jeff. 2022. "The 25 Highest Paying Trade Jobs." *The Interview Guys*. https://theinterviewguys.com/highest-paying-trade-jobs/.

Hogan, C. L., Mata, J., & Carstensen, L. L. (2013). "Exercise holds immediate benefits for affect and cognition in younger and older adults." *Psychology and Aging*, 28(2): 587–594. https://doi.org/10.1037/a00326349.

Jebb, A.T., L. Tay, L. and E. Diener. 2018. "Happiness, income satiation and turning points around the world." *Nature Human Behavior*, no. 2: 33–38. https://doi.org/10.1038/s41562-017-0277-0.

Lawler, K. A., J.W. Younger, R. L. Piferi, E. Billington, R. Jobe, K. Edmondson, and W.H. Jones. 2003. "A change of heart: cardiovascular correlates of forgiveness in response to interpersonal conflict." *Journal of behavioral medicine*, 26(5): 373–393. https://doi.org/10.1023/a:1025771716686.

Lindqvist, P.G., E. Epstein, M. Landin-Olsson, C. Ingvar, K. Nielsen, M. Stenbeck, and H. Olsson. 2014. "Avoidance of sun exposure is a risk factor for all-cause mortality: results from the MISS cohort." *Journal of International Medicine* 86.6: 276-277. https://doi.org/10.1111/joim.12251

"Physical Activity." 2022. *Centers for Disease Control and Prevention,* Centers for Disease Control and Prevention. Last modified 20 May 2022. https://www.cdc.gov/physicalactivity/index.html.

Royal, James F. 2022. "What Is the Average Stock Market Return?" *NerdWallet.* https://www.nerdwallet.com/article/investing/average-stock-market-return.

Tiwari S. C. 2013. Loneliness: A disease?. *Indian journal of psychiatry,* 55(4): 320–322. https://doi.org/10.4103/0019-5545.120536.

U.S. Office of Personnel Management (OPM). N.D. "Alcoholism in the Workplace: A Handbook for Supervisors." https://www.opm.gov/policy-data-oversight/worklife/reference-materials/alcoholism-in-the-workplace-a-handbook-for-supervisors/.

JOIN MY NEWSLETTER

Make sure to sign up to my newsletter for news, updated, and free materials. I will not spam your email and will only send information you may find useful.

◆ ◆ ◆

SIGN UP FOR MY NEWSLETTER HERE:
www.joceyj.com/breakfree-newsletter
(If you scroll all the way to the bottom of the page you can sign up in the footer)

◆ ◆ ◆

Thank you!

- Jocelyn

ACKNOWLEDGEMENT

Thank you to Janessa Bassett, Zac Cavender, Spencer Allen, and Jeremey Maxfield for being beta readers for the book at an early stage. You all provided valuable feedback and helped turn this book into something great.

Thank you to Melissa Powers for making my jargon actually make sense to the average reader. You provided so much value to this book and I really appreciate your work.

Thank you to Kristianto Raharja for taking my super broad idea of a book cover and making it something special. I appreciate your creativity and the amazing book cover you designed.

Thank you to Brady for putting up with me always working to help me with this book. I seriously could not have done it without your help.

Finally, thank you to all my teachers and coaches who I had throughout my life. Without any of you I would not be the person I am today.

ABOUT THE AUTHOR

Jocelyn Kaufman

 Jocelyn was born in the small town of Tooele, Utah. She played softball in college and eventually graduated college to become a high school teacher. Jocelyn retired after 4 years of teaching due to her success in real estate. Jocelyn now has dozens of rentals and has created a life of financial freedom for herself.

Jocelyn now focuses on helping to educate others on how to create financial freedom. She is now a realtor, active investor, co-host of The Break Free Real Estate Podcast, and author of the book Break Free: Design a Life of Financial Freedom where she teaches the reader how to set their life up for financial success.

When she is not busy with real estate Jocelyn is the head softball coach at a high school in Utah. She loves all types of sports and has her purple belt in Brazilian Jiu-Jitsu. Jocelyn loves spending time at home with her bernadoodle puppy and partner.

www.ingramcontent.com/pod-product-compliance
Lightning Source LLC
Chambersburg PA
CBHW071134220526
45467CB00015B/1006